A Textbook of Galactorrhoea
(With an emphasis on Homoeopathic Management)

By
Dr. Rajneesh Kumar Sharma
B.Sc., B.H.M.S., M.D. (Hom), hMD (U.K.),
D.I. Hom. (London), D.Lit. (U.K.), PhD

2024

<u>Dedication</u>

Dedicated

With gratitude and reverence,

To our parents - the architects of our existence!

To our family - the pillars of support that upheld us!

To our colleagues and friends - the steadfast allies who bolstered us!

And

To Homoeopathy - the nurturing embrace that enveloped us!

And

Unified, we merge into its essence!

(Dr. Rajneesh Kumar Sharma)

<u>Acknowledgement</u>

I am deeply grateful to Dr. (Prof. Emeritus) V. K. Khanna for his profound intellect, scientific perspective, continuous guidance, unwavering encouragement, and genuine interest, which have consistently empowered me throughout my research journey. Without his invaluable mentorship, this work would not have been possible. I sincerely appreciate his generosity in sparing time from his busy schedule.

I extend my heartfelt thanks to my colleagues who supported me throughout this endeavor.

I acknowledge the dedication of my friends and colleagues who provided counsel during this period.

Lastly, I express my gratitude to my family, who quietly endured sacrifices to support and enable the completion of this task.

I also extend my thanks to the hospital staff and acquaintances who assisted me in this endeavor.

Dr. Rajneesh Kumar Sharma

<u>Preface</u>

'Galactorrhea' describes the occurrence of milk or milk-like fluid from the breast outside of the postpartum period. While not common, this condition can cause significant mental distress for affected individuals. In newborns, it is usually a natural and temporary phenomenon that may worry unaware parents. In older individuals, especially adolescents or young women, galactorrhea can be emotionally distressing and stigmatizing. Patients often feel reluctant to discuss their symptoms due to shame and fear of a serious underlying cause, leading to ongoing anxiety and uncertainty.

The process of lactation is regulated by various hormones including estrogen, progesterone, and prolactin (PRL), as well as insulin, thyroid hormones, and glucocorticoids. Changes in estrogen and progesterone levels after childbirth facilitate milk production, while unilateral galactorrhea may suggest a localized breast issue such as breast carcinoma. Other potential causes include pituitary disorders, kidney disease, hypothyroidism, and sarcoidosis.

Galactorrhea affects individuals holistically, impacting their mental and physical well-being in unique ways influenced by underlying factors. The interplay of different disease tendencies, known as miasms, can contribute to hormonal imbalances and associated symptoms. For instance, the Psora miasm disrupts physiology, potentially leading to hormonal disturbances, while combinations with other miasms like Syphilis or Sycosis can further complicate the clinical picture.

Understanding galactorrhea requires knowledge of hormone function, breast physiology, and homoeopathic principles. This comprehensive understanding is essential for effective treatment strategies tailored to each patient.

In my exploration of galactorrhea and related topics, I aim to honor the foundational work of historical thinkers and philosophers who paved the way for our modern understanding of these complex issues.

Life presents ongoing challenges rather than permanent solutions, emphasizing the importance of continual research and sharing informed experiences to better define and address patient concerns.

Dr. Rajneesh Kumar Sharma

Contents

Rhea, also known as Cybele, revered as the mother of the Gods

Galactorrhoea- an Overview

Galactorrhea refers to the abnormal discharge of milk from the nipple in non-pregnant females or males. This milk production is unrelated to pregnancy and can have either a physiological or pathological origin. Physiologically-induced secretions typically arise from multiple duct openings, whereas pathologic discharge often stems from a single duct. Other abnormal discharges can result from various pathological causes. The condition is triggered by pituitary gland stimulation, leading to the release of prolactin, which initiates milk production in the breast lobules and ducts.

Between 50% to 80% of women experience nipple discharge at some point during their reproductive years. Approximately 5% of these cases are associated with breast cancer, with higher risks observed in older individuals, particularly those over 40 years of age, especially if the discharge is unilateral, bloody, and from a single duct.

A detailed clinical history indicating endocrine, renal, or hepatic issues should prompt further laboratory assessments. Measurement of serum prolactin levels is recommended for patients reporting headaches, visual disturbances, or menstrual irregularities alongside nipple discharge. Pregnancy testing is also advisable for women of reproductive age experiencing menstrual disturbances.

Differential diagnosis focuses on distinguishing between physiological and pathological causes. Possible diagnoses include pregnancy-related changes, non-milk-related discharge due to friction or manipulation, systemic diseases, pituitary disorders, cancers, ductal ectasia, intraductal papilloma, Paget's disease, eczema, and localized inflammation from trauma or infection.

Physiological discharges are typically multiductal, bilateral, painless, and triggered by stimulation or medication. The color of such discharge can range from white to clear, yellow, or green, with a milky consistency due to pituitary stimulation.

In contrast, pathological discharges are often unilateral, from a single duct, and spontaneous. The color may vary, and blood or pus might be evident. One-third of bloody discharges are associated with cancer, especially in older women with masses present. Benign tumors, infections, or systemic diseases can also cause pathological discharge.

Origin of Words- 'Galact' and 'Rhoea'-

The term "galacto" derives from "galakt," meaning milk, as spoken by the ancient Greeks around 1000 B.C.

Rhea, also known as Cybele, was revered as the mother of the gods, from whom all elements of the universe were believed to emanate. In Roman mythology, Rhea was part of a family of maternal deities, including Cybele, Ceres (or Demeter), and others. These figures inspired various attributes that influenced words and concepts such as cereal, ceremony, cerebral, materialism, matrimony, and matter, as explored in different contexts. Here, our focus is on Rhea's connection to terms like Rhesus, Rhine, Galactorrhea, Pyorrhea, Diarrhea, Rhinorrhea, and more distantly related concepts such as flow, fluid, flight, river, and renal.

Rhea evokes the ancient Hindu concept of creation, where the gods and demons united in a rare collaboration to seek immortality by churning an ocean of milk. This primordial ocean, thought to originate from the galactic or milky galaxies, flowed forth as the Ganga (Ganges) river. Legend has it that Ganga descended from the heavens and was caught in the matted hair of Shiva, diffusing its force into gentle rivers and streams, including the sacred Ganges.

On a more practical level, terms like "rhea" and "rhein" symbolize the essence of flow, particularly that of rivers and streams. This association extends to the rhesus monkey (Macaca mulatta), known for its affinity for swimming in rivers. Interestingly, this species shares with humans an antigen factor called Rh. In the 1940s, researchers identified a hemolytic anemia in fetuses or newborns caused by Rh antigenic incompatibility with the mother, coining the term "Rh disease" to describe this condition.

Rhea or Cybele

In medical terminology, abnormal fluid flow into diseased tissues is characterized as "rheuma" or "rheumatism," encompassing conditions like rheumatic fever and related ailments. This interconnectedness of language and concepts underscores the rich historical and scientific narrative surrounding the origins and implications of these terms.

"Birth of the Milky Way" Sketch by P. Rubens- Prado Museum Madrid, Spain
(Shown is Hera who trying to nurse Hercules. Apparently, he was so strong that he bit her nipple, which forced her to disengage him and to spill her breast milk.)

Galactorrhea can occur in both males and females. The phenomenon of male lactation was initially documented among survivors of Nazi concentration camps after World War II. Additionally, some

                                    Dr. Rajneesh Kumar Sharma

American prisoners of war returning from the Korean and Vietnam Wars reported experiencing male lactation. In both males and females, it is possible to induce lactation through consistent nipple massage and simulated 'sucking' over an extended period.

Interestingly, male lactation is observed in one non-human species, the Dayak fruit bat (Dyacopterus spadiceus), where lactating males contribute to infant nursing.

Historically, the Talmud records a case of a man who nursed his infant following his wife's untimely death, likely one of the earliest documented instances of male galactorrhea. The medical understanding of galactorrhea and its association with amenorrhea dates back to the 19th century, notably described by Chiari. However, it wasn't until the 1950s that Argonz and colleagues, as well as Forbes and colleagues, linked galactorrhea and amenorrhea to pituitary tumors and prolactin (PRL) levels.

Ancient Medical Writings: Breast Health in Early Texts

Throughout history, breasts have held symbolic significance in art, religion, and legend due to their association with fertility and the nurturing provision of life-giving milk. Prehistoric female figurines, such as the Venus of Willendorf or the "Snake Goddess" of Minoan civilization, often prominently feature emphasized breasts, underscoring their symbolic importance.

Minoan Snake Goddess (Venus of Willendorf) from the Palace at Knossos- Crete and Goddess Artemis, too many breasts to count

In ancient times, goddesses like Artemis were depicted with multiple breasts, symbolizing their role as protectors of childbirth and motherhood. Various religions have also ascribed special significance to the breast, whether through formal teachings or symbolic representation. This enduring cultural and spiritual connection highlights the profound symbolism attached to this aspect of human anatomy across diverse civilizations and belief systems.

People have been intrigued by the anatomy and physiology of the breast for thousands of years. Ancient Greek and Roman medical writings by Hippocrates, Soranus, and Galen included discussions on infant health and feeding as part of their broader treatises on health. These concepts were carried forward into the Middle Ages by scholars of the Arabian School such as Rhazes, Avicenna, and Averroes, and later reemerged in the works of Renaissance medical writers like Bagellardus, Metlinger, Roesslin, Phayer, Muffet, and de Vallambert, leaving a lasting impact on pediatric literature.

Earliest Medical Writings: Ancient Egyptian Insights

The earliest known medical writings about breast health can be traced back to ancient Egypt. These writings described methods to assess the quality of a mother's milk and techniques to increase milk supply. Recommendations included back rubs with fish-infused oil and breast massages using a poppy plant while sitting cross-legged. While these methods likely helped relax nursing mothers, they probably had little direct effect on milk production, as noted by modern commentators like Marilyn Yalom.

Hippocrates (460-377 BC): Menstrual Blood and Human Milk

Hippocrates, the ancient physician, proposed a unique theory that menstrual blood was transformed into human milk. This belief persisted for centuries, influencing medical thought on breastfeeding and lactation until the 17th century. The enduring legacy of Hippocrates reflects the ongoing curiosity and evolving understanding of breast physiology throughout history.

Hippocrates

Leonardo da Vinci's (1452-1519) Anatomical Discoveries

Leonardo da Vinci made groundbreaking anatomical observations in his sketches. Among his notable discoveries, da Vinci depicted veins connecting the uterus directly to the breasts in his detailed anatomical drawings.

Da Vinci's sketches, characterized by their precision and anatomical accuracy, reflected his keen observation skills and deep interest in understanding human anatomy. His depiction of venous connections between the uterus and breasts was a significant anatomical insight that contributed to the evolving understanding of reproductive physiology during the Renaissance period.

Leonardo da Vinci's anatomical studies continue to inspire and inform modern scientific investigations, highlighting the enduring legacy of his contributions to medical science and art.

Leonardo Da Vinci

Aristotle's (384-822 BC) Views on Breastfeeding

The philosopher Aristotle shared his insights on breastfeeding, reflecting the beliefs of his time. He suggested that darker-skinned women produced healthier milk compared to fair-skinned women, a notion rooted in ancient perceptions of bodily humors and skin color.

Aristotle

Aristotle also speculated that infants who consumed warmer mother's milk tended to develop teeth at an earlier age — an observation influenced by empirical observations rather than scientific evidence.

One notable misconception attributed to Aristotle is his view that infants should not consume colostrum, the nutrient-rich first milk produced by mothers after childbirth. This misconception has persisted in some cultures despite modern medical knowledge affirming the importance of colostrum for newborns' health and development.

Aristotle's reflections on breastfeeding offer valuable insights into the historical understanding of infant care and the complexities of early medical theories.

Soranus (100-140 AD): Insights on Milk Supply Remedies

Soranus, an ancient gynecologist, offered insights into remedies for low milk supply in breastfeeding mothers. He suggested that breast massage and self-induced vomiting could potentially aid in increasing milk production.

However, Soranus dismissed the effectiveness of certain remedies, such as "drinks mixed with the ashes of burnt owls and bats," highlighting the diverse range of practices and beliefs surrounding ancient medical treatments.

Soranus' contributions underscore the historical evolution of medical knowledge and the complexities of ancient therapeutic approaches, reflecting the cultural and scientific context of his time.

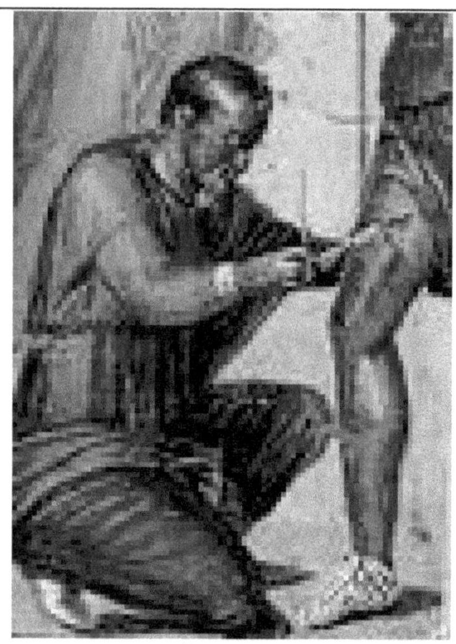

Soranus

Avicenna (980-1037 AD): Contributions to Medicine

Avicenna, also known as Ibn Sina or al-Shaykh al Rais, was a renowned Persian Muslim physician, scientist, and philosopher. In his seminal work, "The Canon of Medicine," written in 1012 AD, Avicenna made significant contributions to medical knowledge by classifying and describing various diseases.

His comprehensive text covered a wide range of medical conditions, including diabetes, tuberculosis, and brain diseases such as tumors. Avicenna's meticulous classification and detailed descriptions of diseases represented a major advancement in medical understanding during the medieval period.

Avicenna's enduring legacy in medicine continues to inspire and inform modern medical practices, highlighting his profound impact on the development of medical science in the Islamic Golden Age and beyond.

Avicenna

It proposes causes for diseases, suggesting that tuberculosis is contagious. It also outlines treatments for diseases and methods of hygiene.

Vesalius (1514 AD) and the Advancement of Anatomy

In the 16th century, anatomists like Vesalius made significant strides in understanding human anatomy. Through meticulous dissections of cadavers, they discovered that breasts were composed of glandular tissue. This led them to hypothesize that the glandular tissue "converts the blood brought to them by the veins into milk."

Vesalius' observations and reasoning marked a pivotal moment in the history of anatomical study, laying the foundation for a more accurate understanding of the physiological processes underlying lactation and breast function. His contributions exemplify the growing importance of empirical research and anatomical investigation during the Renaissance period.

Vesalius

Wet Nurses: Historical Perspectives

The practice of wet nursing, where lactating women were hired to breastfeed another woman's baby, has

 Dr. Rajneesh Kumar Sharma

been documented in early writings spanning diverse cultures. References to wet nursing can be found in ancient texts such as the Code of Hammurabi, the Bible, the Quran, and the works of Homer, among others. These writings often expressed opinions on what characteristics made the best wet nurses, including considerations like hair color, breast appearance, and whether the woman had previously borne male or female children.

During the 1700s, medical understanding evolved to recognize the health benefits of a mother nursing her own child over employing a wet nurse. There was also a growing appreciation for the importance of newborns receiving colostrum, the initial nutrient-rich milk produced by mothers after childbirth.

Colostrum and Milk Studies: Modern Insights

In recent decades, medical science has made significant strides in understanding human milk, particularly in immunology. We now understand that colostrum is rich in antibodies that protect newborns from diseases, while mature milk provides optimal nutrition for infants. As toddlers nurse less frequently, the concentration of immune factors in their mother's milk increases.

Furthermore, studies have shown that milk composition varies between mothers and even within the same mother from day to day and throughout the day. The Womanly Art of Breastfeeding highlights this variability, emphasizing that each mother's milk is unique and tailored to meet her baby's changing needs.

Al-Razi (865-925 AD): Contributions to Medicine

Al-Razi, also known as Rhazes, was a distinguished physician, philosopher, and alchemist. His extensive medical writings, organized anatomically from head to toe, synthesized knowledge from diverse sources. Al-Razi's clinical observations often challenged prevailing opinions, providing valuable insights that enriched medical understanding during his time and beyond. His contributions laid the groundwork for advancements in medicine and anatomy, exemplifying the spirit of scientific inquiry and critical thinking in medieval scholarship.

Al Razi

STUDIES RELATED TO THE HYPOTHALAMUS AND PITUITARY

The term "hypothalamus" originates from Greek, where "hypo" means below and "thalamus" refers to bed, indicating its anatomical position beneath the thalamus in all vertebrates.

Galen's Contributions

Galen, a prominent physician in ancient Rome, provided early insights into the hypothalamus and pituitary gland.

He described the hypothalamic infundibulum as well as the pituitary gland, likening them to a draining route and receptacle, respectively, for mucus passing from the brain's ventricular structures to the nasopharynx.

Galen named the capillary network surrounding the pituitary gland the "rete mirabilis."

His concepts dominated scientific understanding of the hypothalamus and pituitary for approximately 1200 years, reflecting the enduring influence of his observations in the history of neuroscience.

Galen and His Works

A- De naturalibus facultatibus libri tres. B- The decoration to the left of the title as well as the historiated initial "Q" are quite similar to that of the 1534 Razi, also printed in Paris but at a different printer's house. C- Historiated initial with angel, arrow and man in the moon, and the marginalia.

Dr. Rajneesh Kumar Sharma

Mondino de' Liuzzi's Contributions to Anatomy

In the 14th century, the Italian anatomist Mondino de' Liuzzi made significant contributions to the understanding of brain anatomy in his work titled "Anathomia." Mondino proposed that the third ventricle of the brain functions as an "integrator" of body functions.

Description of the functional role exerted by the cerebral third ventricle, as reported by Mondino de' Liuzzi in Anothomia

(A) Original FrontPage of Anothomia in a XIV century edition (B) Original text (in brackets) in medieval Latin (The 1316 CE manuscript kept at the Società Medica Chirurgica in Bologna, Italy) (C) A portion of the Latin fragment shown in (B) containing the most important concepts; (D) English translation shown in (B) (Toni R., Ancient views on the hypothalamic-pituitary-thyroid axis: an historical and epistemological perspective, Pituitary 3: 83-95, 2000)

Mondino's pioneering insight into the role of the third ventricle as an integrative center for coordinating bodily functions was a remarkable advance in neuroscience for his time. His work laid the foundation for further exploration into the complex interactions within the brain and the regulation of physiological processes. Mondino's anatomical studies exemplify the early roots of neuroscience and the quest to comprehend the intricacies of human anatomy and function.

Leonardo da Vinci's Exploration of Brain Anatomy

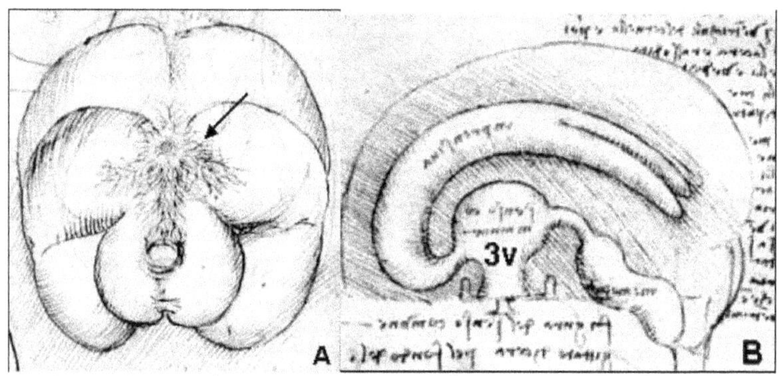

Drawings of Brain Anatomy by Leonardo da Vinci (1508-1509)

(A) Inferior surface of the brain, showing the rete mirabilis (arrow) that surrounds the pituitary gland (Codici di Anatomia of the Windsor's Collectio - Courtesy of the Library of the Department of Human Anatomy of the University of Parma, Italy) (B) 3-D representation of the cerebral ventricles. The third ventricle (3v) as believed to be the site of afference and laboration of the sensus communis" (Latin for peripheral physical sensations)

Leonardo da Vinci, renowned for his multifaceted genius, delved into the study of brain anatomy with remarkable depth and precision. Inspired by Vesalius and other anatomists of his time, Leonardo's detailed drawings included depictions of the third ventricle and the rete mirabile (miraculous network of blood vessels).

Leonardo's sketches of the brain's internal structures, including the intricate network of blood vessels surrounding the pituitary gland, reflected his keen observational skills and artistic mastery. These drawings, now regarded as significant historical artifacts, provided valuable insights into the understanding of brain anatomy during the Renaissance period.

Leonardo da Vinci's contributions to brain anatomy exemplify the convergence of art and science, showcasing his innovative approach to anatomical illustration and his enduring impact on the field of neuroscience.

Andreas Vesalius: Advancements in Anatomical Illustration

Andreas Vesalius, a pioneering figure in anatomical study during the 16th century, expanded upon earlier ideas with groundbreaking discoveries. In his seminal work, "De Humani Corporis Fabrica," first published in 1543, Vesalius presented the first anatomical depiction of the infundibular-pituitary stalk in Book 7.

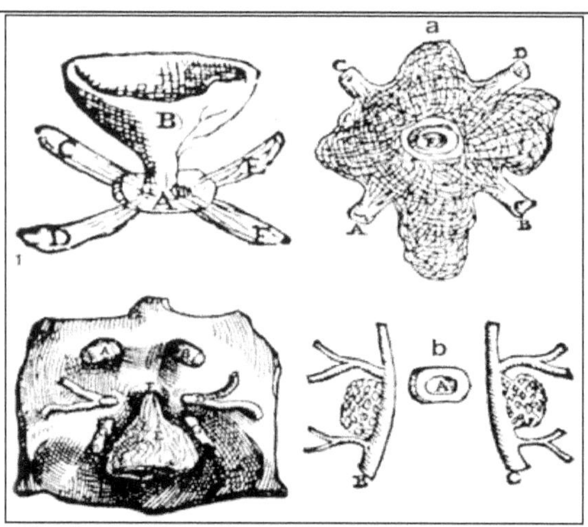

(Andreas Vesalius-Plates from Fabrica)

Showing what is believed to be the oldest anatomical images in Western literature of the hypothalamic-pituitary unit. (Courtesy of the Library of the Department of Human Anatomy of the University of Bologna, Italy, with permission.) 1) Enlarged view of the pituitary gland (A), hypothalamic infundibulum (B) and ducts comprising the foramen lacerum and superior orbital fissure (C, D, E, F) believed to drain the brain mucus or phlegm (in Latin pituita) from the pituitary gland to the nasopharynx; 2) anatomical relationships between the infundibulum (D), the dural diaphragma sellae (F), the internal carotid arteries (C, D) and occulomotor nerves (G); 3) composite image including a) an enlarged view of the rete mirabilis formed as a reticular plexus by the carotid arteries entering (A, B) and emerging (C, D) around the pituitary gland (E); b) detailed view of the reticular plexus arising from the carotids (B, C) on each side of the pituitary (A).

Vesalius' meticulous illustrations and detailed descriptions revolutionized anatomical understanding,

    Dr. Rajneesh Kumar Sharma

setting new standards for accuracy and scientific inquiry. His depiction of the infundibular-pituitary stalk represented a significant milestone in the exploration of brain anatomy and endocrine function.

The publication of "De Humani Corporis Fabrica" marked a watershed moment in the history of medicine, solidifying Vesalius' reputation as a trailblazer in anatomical illustration and laying the groundwork for future discoveries in the field of anatomy and physiology.

Michelangelo Buonarroti (1475-1564): Artistic Representation of Brain Anatomy

Michelangelo Buonarroti, renowned for his masterpiece on the ceiling of the Sistine Chapel in the Vatican at Rome, ingeniously utilized the hypothalamic-pituitary region as a backdrop for his depiction of the creation of man. The intricacies of this region, woven into the artistic narrative of creation, highlight Michelangelo's visionary approach to integrating anatomical motifs into his art.

Scientific Advancements in Hypothalamic-Pituitary Understanding

The discovery of the connection between the hypothalamus and posterior pituitary gland, known as the supraoptic-hypophysial tract, by Ramon Cajal in 1894 marked a pivotal moment in neuroscience. Subsequent research on neurosecretion in the fish hypothalamus by the Sharrers in 1928 furthered our understanding of neuroendocrine signaling.

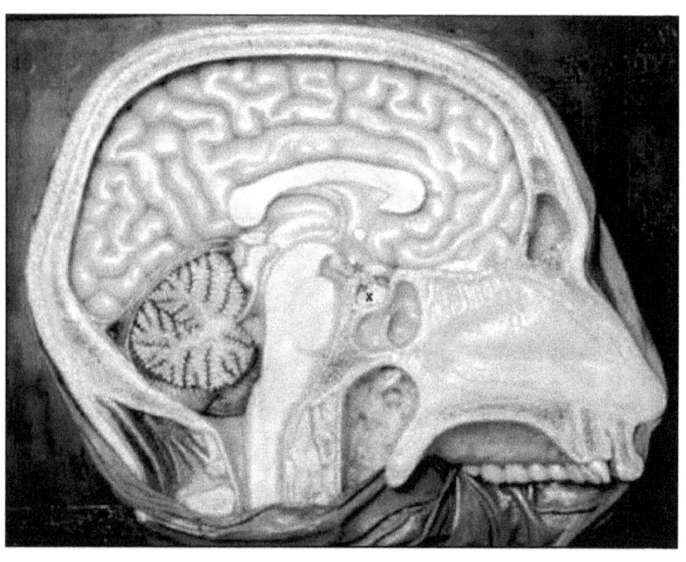

Midsaggital section of the human brain
(From the XIX century wax collection of human brains at the Museum of the Department of Human Anatomy of the University of Bologna, Italy). The hypothalamus (asterisk) lies above the pituitary gland (cross) and has as its boundaries (1) the anterior commissure and lamina terminalis anteriorly; (2) mammillary bodies and midbrain posteriorly, and (3) thalamus uperiorly.
(From Lechan R.M. and Toni R., Regulation of Pituitary Function, in Korenman S.G (Ed), Atlas of Clinical Endocrinology, Current Medicine, vol IV, 1-25, 2000).

These foundational discoveries laid the groundwork for rapid advancements in hypothalamic research throughout the 20th century and into the 21st century.

The evolving exploration of the hypothalamus continues to deepen our understanding of its vital role in regulating physiological processes and hormone secretion, bridging the realms of art and science in the quest for knowledge about the human brain.

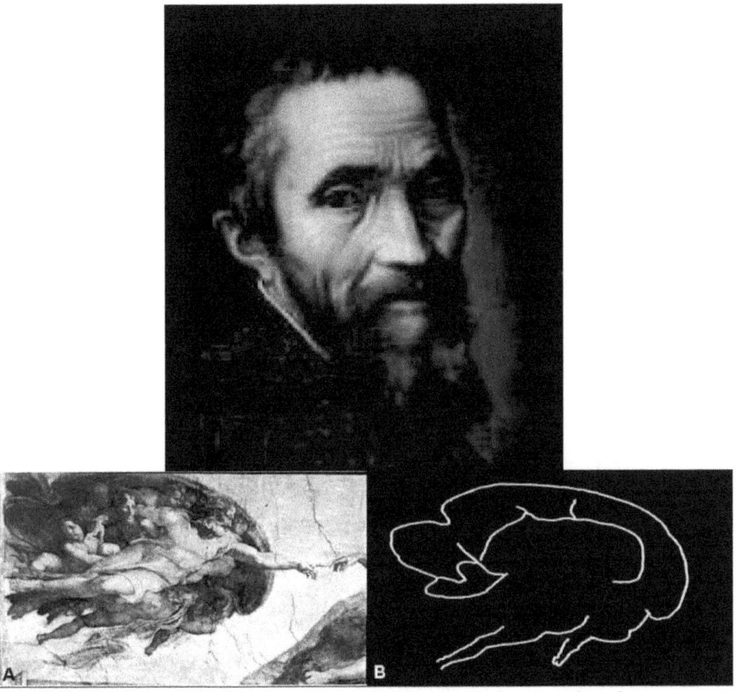

Michelangelo Buonarroti- Detail from the fresco, "Creation of Adam

" It is visible on the ceiling of the Sistine Chapel in the Vatican at Rome, Italy, painted between 1508-1512. Photograph of the fresco showing God giving spiritual life and intellect to Adam through his touch (B) The contour of the same image is reminiscent of a midline saggital section of the brain and includes the hypothalamus, pituitary and brainstem.

Timeline of Key Discoveries in Mammalian Hypothalamic-Pituitary Anatomy

- **2nd Century CE**: Galen describes the hypothalamic infundibulum and pituitary gland as routes for brain mucous drainage, noting the existence of the "rete mirabilis."
- **1316**: Mondino dei Liuzzi in "Anothomia" refers to the third cerebral ventricle as an "integrator" of body functions.
- **1522**: Berangario da Carpi denies the existence of Galenic "rete mirabilis" in the human brain.
- **1543**: Vesalius includes the first anatomical drawings of the hypothalamic infundibulum and pituitary in "Fabrica."
- **1561-1527**: Fallopius and Casserio mention the arterial polygon at the brain base, later described by Willis.
- **1664**: Willis argues that humors from the third ventricle may reach the pituitary gland.
- **1655-1672**: Schneider and Lower reject the idea of the pituitary gland filtering brain secretions to the nose.
- **1742**: Lieutand discovers vessels in the pituitary stalk.
- **1778**: Sommering introduces-term "hypophysis."
- **1860**: Von Luska describes the primary (or hypothalamic) capillary plexus of portal vessels.
- **1872-1877**: Meynert and Forel define the anatomical borders of the hypothalamus.
- **1893**: His introduces the term "hypothalamus" and provides the first anatomical subdivision based on human brain ontogenesis.

- **1894**: Ramon Y. Cajal discovers the connection between the hypothalamus and posterior pituitary in rats (supraoptico-hypophysial tract).
- **1928**: E. Scharrer describes "glandular cells" in the fish hypothalamus, introducing the concept of "neurosecretion."
- **1930**: Popa and Fielding describe a portal vascular system in the human pituitary stalk.
- **1940-1955**: Harris and Green establish neural control of pituitary gland secretion and demonstrate its vascular link with hypothalamus.
- **1950-1958**: Nauta and Kuypers propose that the limbic system influences pituitary function, introducing "hypothalamic integration."
- **1960**: Martinez describes the structure of the median eminence.
- **1962**: Halaz introduces the concept of the "hypophysiotrophic area" of the hypothalamus.
- **1964**: Szentagothi defines the tuberoinfundibular tract.
- **1968**: Guillemin and Schally isolate the first hypothalamic releasing factor.
- **1970**: Nakane provides ultrastructural evidence for paracrine interactions in the pituitary gland.

This timeline reflects the progressive unraveling of mammalian hypothalamic-pituitary anatomy through centuries of scientific inquiry, laying the foundation for our current understanding of neuroendocrine regulation and hormone secretion mechanisms.

Classical thinkers such as Aristotle, Hippocrates, Lucretius, Celsus, and Galen laid foundational ideas about health and disease, often relying on a humoral theory of biological function that seemed logical and practical for their time.

John Hunter (1728-1793): Early Experiments in Endocrinology

John Hunter, a prominent surgeon and anatomist, conducted pioneering experiments in endocrinology during the 18th century. In 1767, Hunter performed deliberate testicular transplantation by transferring a cock's testis into the abdominal cavity of a hen. Despite the testis adhering to the intestine or peritoneum, no significant systemic changes were observed in the recipient hen.

John Hunter

Hunter's experiment, although not yielding expected results in hormone function, marked an important step in understanding the principles of tissue transplantation. His focus on transplantation techniques laid groundwork for future investigations in endocrinology and organ transplantation, contributing to the broader understanding of hormonal function in biological systems.

Arnold Berthold (1801-1863): Pioneer of Hormone Research

Arnold Berthold made foundational contributions to the study of hormones in 1849 when he discovered that secondary sexual characteristics were markedly altered after grafting of testes or castration in chick and cockerels. Berthold's experiments highlighted the role of testicular function in influencing physiological changes, laying the groundwork for understanding endocrine regulation.

Claude Bernard (12th July 1813 - 10th Feb 1878): Advancing the Concept of Internal Secretion

In 1855, Claude Bernard introduced the term "internal secretion" for the first time, emphasizing the concept of glands secreting substances directly into the bloodstream to exert systemic effects.

Claude Bernard

Bernard's work elucidated the significance of internal secretions in regulating bodily functions, contributing significantly to the development of endocrinology and hormonal studies.

Thomas Addison (April 1793 - June 29, 1860): Pioneering Endocrinologist

In 1855, Thomas Addison made a groundbreaking discovery that revolutionized the field of endocrinology. He identified a syndrome characterized by adrenal cortex destruction, now known as "Addison's Disease." This syndrome, marked by adrenal insufficiency, is named in honor of Addison's seminal contribution to medical science.

Thomas Addison is rightfully recognized as the "Father of Endocrinology" for his pivotal role in elucidating the relationship between adrenal function and health. His discovery laid the foundation for understanding adrenal hormone production and the broader field of endocrine disorders.

Thomas Addison

Charles Edouard Brown-Séquard (1817-1894): Contributions to Endocrinology

Charles Edouard Brown-Séquard's 1856 study on the effects of adrenal gland extirpation in animals marked a significant milestone in endocrinology.

Charles Edouard Brown-Séquard

His research led him to believe that beyond the testes, other organs such as the thyroid, adrenal glands, pancreas, liver, spleen, and kidneys also secreted substances with potential therapeutic value.

Brown-Séquard's pioneering work laid the groundwork for exploring the endocrine functions of various organs and their potential applications in medical treatments. His insights into organ secretions paved the way for further discoveries in endocrinology, highlighting the diverse roles of hormones and their impact on health and disease.

William Bayliss (1860-1924) and Ernest Starling (17th April 1866, London - 2nd May 1927, Jamaica): Pioneers of Hormonal Research

The modern concept of hormones was established by William Bayliss and Ernest Starling through their groundbreaking experiments conducted between 1902 and 1905. In 1905, Starling coined the term "hormone" to describe what he referred to as an "exciting substance."

Bayliss and Starling, both professors from the Department of Physiology at University College London, extracted a unique substance from duodenal mucosa in 1902. They named this substance "secretin" and discovered that when injected into the bloodstream, secretin stimulated the secretion of water and bicarbonate by a denervated pancreas.

Ernest Starling photographed in his office around 1921
(The three-piece suit and the wing collar were his
uniform throughout the 1920s.)

Similar to Berthold's earlier work, Bayliss and Starling
proposed that chemical secretion, rather than nervous
control, was responsible for the physiological effects
they observed. They further hypothesized that these
chemical messengers, circulating in the blood and
acting on distant target tissues, could regulate a wide
range of bodily functions.

The experiments and concepts introduced by Bayliss
and Starling laid the foundation for the understanding
of hormones as signaling molecules that regulate
physiological processes, shaping the field of
endocrinology and modern medicine.

William B. Hardy (1864-1934): Introduction of the Term "Hormone"

William B. Hardy, a Cambridge physiologist, played a pivotal role in the naming of hormones during a visit to the laboratory of William Bayliss and Ernest Starling. Inspired by their groundbreaking work, Hardy proposed the term "hormone," derived from a Greek word meaning "I arouse to activity" or "setting something in motion." On June 20th, 1905, Ernest Starling used the term "hormone" for the first time to describe the exciting substances identified by Bayliss and Starling in their experiments on secretin and other physiological regulators.

William B. Hardy

Hardy's contribution in naming hormones not only provided a concise and evocative term for these regulatory substances but also symbolized the dynamic role of hormones in orchestrating biological activities within the body. This milestone marked the formal recognition of hormones as vital messengers in physiological processes.

<u>STUDIES RELATED TO HOMOEOPATHY</u>

The Origins and Principles of Homeopathy

The term "homeopathy" is derived from two Greek words: "homois," meaning similar, and "pathos," meaning suffering. Homeopathy refers to a therapeutic approach that involves treating diseases with remedies prescribed in minute doses, which are capable of producing symptoms similar to the disease when taken by healthy individuals. This method is based on the natural law of healing known as "Similia Similibus Curantur," which translates to "like cures like."

Dr. Christian Friedrich Samuel Gottfried Hahnemann (1755-1843) established homeopathy on a scientific basis in the early 19th century. Over two centuries, homeopathy has served suffering humanity and has proven its efficacy despite the passage of time and changing medical practices. The scientific principles articulated by Dr. Hahnemann are rooted in nature and have been consistently successful in practice.

Homeopathy continues to be a time-tested therapy that emphasizes individualized treatment and holistic healing, embodying the principle that similar symptoms can be alleviated by substances that produce similar symptoms in healthy individuals. This approach remains a valuable and enduring alternative in healthcare.

Dr. Christian Friedrich Samuel Gottfried Hahnemann

The Evolution and Practice of Homeopathy

Homeopathy has become a rapidly growing healthcare system practiced almost worldwide, with India notably embracing it as a household name due to the safety and gentle nature of its remedies. A rough estimate suggests that around 10% of the Indian population relies solely on homeopathy for their healthcare needs.

In India, homeopathy has deep roots dating back over a century and a half. It has seamlessly integrated into the country's traditions and is recognized as one of the National Systems of Medicine, playing a crucial role in providing healthcare to a significant portion of the population. Its strength lies in its evident effectiveness, employing a holistic approach that promotes inner balance at mental, emotional, spiritual, and physical levels.

Origin of Homeopathy

The principles of homeopathy trace back to Hippocrates from ancient Greece, the father of medicine, around 450 BC. Over a thousand years later, the Swiss alchemist Paracelsus employed a similar healing system based on the principle of "like cures like." However, it was in the late 18th century that homeopathy, as practiced today, was developed by the renowned German physician, Dr. Samuel Hahnemann.

Dr. Hahnemann was deeply dissatisfied with the medical practices of his time and sought to create a method of healing that was safe, gentle, and effective.

He believed in the inherent healing capacity of human beings and viewed disease symptoms as manifestations of the body's effort to overcome illness.

Over two hundred years ago, Dr. Hahnemann discovered the principle that a substance capable of causing symptoms in a healthy individual could also cure those same symptoms in a sick person. His revelation came while studying the effects of Cinchona Bark, which contains quinine. Upon taking Cinchona Bark himself, he experienced symptoms identical to intermittent fever (now known as malaria), leading him to theorize that Cinchona worked against this fever because it induced similar symptoms in a healthy individual.

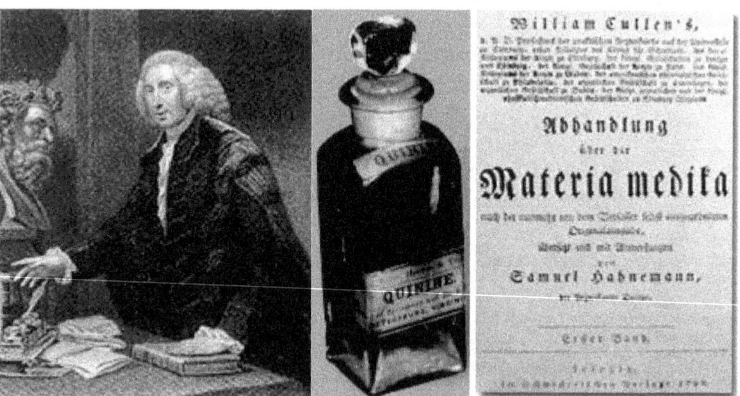

Dr. Cullen, Pharmaceutical Bottle of Quinine used by Hahnemann and Front Page of Cullen's Materia Medica

This insight, sparked by translating Dr. William Cullen's works in 1789, laid the foundation for homeopathy — a unique system of medicine based on

                                   Dr. Rajneesh Kumar Sharma

nature's law of cure. Homeopathy treats the person as a whole, addressing underlying imbalances rather than isolated symptoms or organs, hence its designation as a holistic system of treatment.

Dr. Hahnemann's Groundbreaking Experiments

Dr. Hahnemann continued his experiments, meticulously noting that every substance he ingested — whether it was an herb, a mineral, an animal product, or a chemical compound — produced distinct and specific symptoms in his body. What fascinated him even more was the realization that no two substances elicited the exact same set of symptoms. Each substance provoked its own unique pattern of physical, mental, and emotional symptoms.

Dr. Hahnemann's observations transcended mere physical effects; he also noted profound impacts on the mind and emotions. It was from these detailed experiments and observations that Dr. Hahnemann formulated the principle of "let likes be treated by likes." This foundational concept led him to pioneer the practice of treating illnesses with substances that could produce similar symptoms in healthy individuals.

From the very beginning of applying this principle in clinical practice, Dr. Hahnemann achieved remarkable success. His approach, grounded in the principle of similia similibus curentur (like cures like), revolutionized medical treatment and laid the groundwork for the holistic and individualized approach that defines homeopathy today.

however, well known to physicians, that the most considerable instance of the sympathy mentioned above, is afforded by the stomach, so connected with almost every other part of the system, that motions excited there are communicated to almost every other part of the body, and produce peculiar effects in those parts, however distant from the stomach itself. This indeed is very well known; but that the effects of many medicines which appear in other parts of the body are entirely owing to an action upon the stomach, and that the most part of medicines acting upon the system act immediately upon the stomach only, is what has not been understood till very lately, and does not seem even yet to be very generally and fully perceived by the writers on the materia medica. It will, therefore, be proper here to say in what manner this doctrine may be established.

" *First :* That medicines shewing considerable powers with respect to the whole system, act especially or only on the stomach, will appear from all those cases in which the effects appear soon after the substance has been taken into the stomach, and before they can be supposed to have gone further into the body, or to have reached the mass of blood. Thus, Sir John Pringle, from the sudden operation of the Peruvian bark in preventing the paroxysms of intermittent fevers, properly concludes, that it cannot be by its antiseptic powers with respect to the fluids, but by a certain operation immediately upon the stomach. (See Diseases of the Army, Appendix, p. xxv.)

" *Secondly :* As medicines are commonly in the first place applied to the stomach, so all those of volatile, active, and penetrating parts, must immediately and especially act upon the stomach; and from this consideration, as well as from the suddenness of their effects which commonly appear, we may conclude their action to be upon the stomach only. Accordingly, I conclude that the action of the volatile alkali, and some other saline substances, is upon the stomach alone, and very rarely by any antiseptic powers with respect to the fluids.

" *Thirdly :* Though medicines do not to the taste or smell discover any volatile or active parts, yet if their effects depend upon the change which they produce in the state of the nervous power, it is hardly to be doubted that they operate only

Page No. 151 of Cullen's Materia Medica showing Cinchona Pharmacology
(Adopted from The Works of Willium Cullen by John Thomson- Edinburgh)

Hahnemann divided sickness into-

1- **Indisposition-** slight alteration in the state of health manifested by one or more trivial symptoms. Slight alteration in diet or/and regimen will dispel it.

2- **Surgical diseases-** the diseases with gross pathological, often irreversible changes.

3- **Dynamic diseases-** the diseases due to functional derangement of normal hormony of health, often reversible.

    A. **Acute Diseases-** any disease or illness which can disturb the health of a person temporarily in a negative way. They are rapid in course, intense in pain and severity, short or moderate in duration and end in recovery or death.

        a. **Individual-** occurring only in one individual at a time with different group of symptoms.

        b. **Sporadic-** attacking several persons at a time in different localities with somewhat similar symptoms. viz. Viral Fever, Influenza, Dysentery, Typhoid etc.

        c. **Endemic-** diseases prevalent in a particular locality due to some local circumstances.

        d. **Epidemic-** attacking a large numbr of persons of a vast area at a time with similar set of symptoms.

            i. **Immunizing-** occur only once in the life time of an individual, profylacting against second attack. viz. Small pox, Chicken pox, Measles, Whooping Cough, Scarlet Fever, Mumps etc..

            ii. **Non immunizing-** may occur several times in life of an individual. viz. Cholera, Plague, Yellow Fever,   Diphtheria etc.

e. **Pandemic-** attacking a large area of the world with similar symptoms. viz. influenza.
B. **Chronic diseases-** the diseases appearing incidiously, running indefinitely and leaving life long conseqences or terminating in death, often based on activities of one or more miams, the fundamental causes of all the chronic diseases.
   a. **Artificial-** iatrogenic diseases. i.e. diseases due to excessive use of drugs.
   b. **Inappropriately named chronic diseases-** false chronic diseses, persisting due to some maintaing cause. viz. occupational diseases; bad habits, dust exposure etc.
   c. **True Natural or Miasmatic diseases-** chronic diseases with constitutional signs and symptoms.
      i. **One sided diseases-** having very few perceptive symptoms.
         a) **Internal-** affection of an internal kind, viz. chronic headache or diarrhea.
         b) **External-** affection of an external kind localized in one part only, viz. venous stasis, varicose veins etc.
      ii. **Diseases with full developed symptoms-** these are full fledged chronic diseases.
         a) **Single diseases-** having only one miasm at a time.
            i. **Psora-** the functional miasm causing disturbances in physiology only.
            ii. **Sycosis-** the mal-growth miasm, causing exfoliations, tumorization etc.

    iii. **Syphilis-** the degenerating miasm, causing destructions.

b) **Compound Diseases-** diseases having combination of the more than one miasms.

    i. **Psora-sycosis-** abnormal growths. viz. tumors, keloids etc.

    ii. **Psora-syphilis-** also called Pseudopsora, or Tubercular miasm, causing tubercular degenerations etc. viz. phthisis etc.

    iii. **Syco-syphilis-** causing cystic degenerations. viz. Tubo-ovarian mass etc.

    iv. **Psora-syco-syphilis-** also called cancerous miasm, causing worst forms of diseases like cancer.

PITUITARY GLAND- ANATOMY & PHYSIOLOGY

Location

The pituitary gland lies within a recess of the median part of the middle cranial fossa in the sphenoid bone (sella turcica).

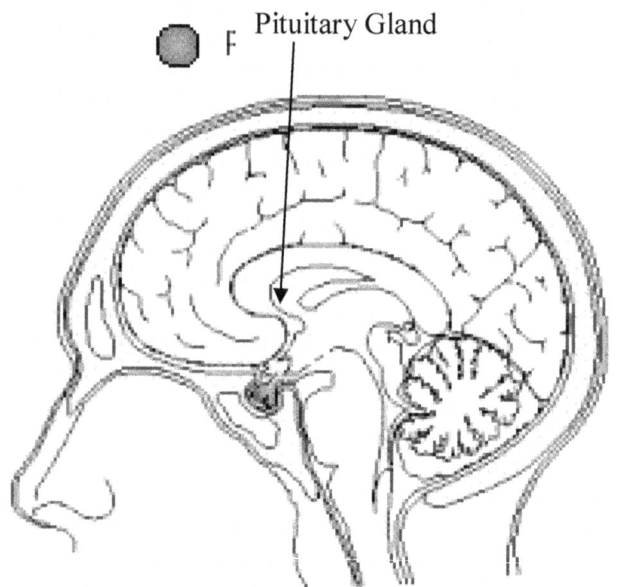

Anatomic Location of Pituitary Gland

Gross Anatomy

It is composed of two major and on minor components-
- Anterior lobe (adenohypophysis)
- Intermediate lobe (rudimentry)
- Posterior lobe (neurohypophysis)

The anterior lobe contains three subdivisions including-

- **Pars distalis-** It makes up the bulk of the anterior pituitary and is primarily responsible for the secretion of anterior pituitary hormones into the peripheral circulation.
- **Pars intermedia-** It lies between the pars distalis and the posterior pituitary and is vestigial in man.
- **Pars tuberalis-** It is well defined in most mammalian species and surrounds the infundibular stem.

Microscopic Anatomy

The anterior pituitary is composed of three types of cells-

1- **Acidophils-** these stain with acidic dyes and secrete GH and PRL.
2- **Basophils-** these stain with basic dyes and secrete LH, FSH, ACTH and TSH.
3- **Chromophobes-** these do not stain with either and supposed to be nonsectretory.

The anterior pituitary is composed of nests or cords of cuboidal cells organized near venous sinusoids lined with a fenestrated epithelium into which secretary products from the anterior pituitary are collected. Classically, five cell types and six secretary products of the anterior pituitary gland can be identified immunocytochemically including-

1- The somatotrophs (growth hormone)
2- Lactotrophs (prolactin)
3- Corticotrophs (adrenocorticotropic hormone)
4- Thyrotropes (thyroid-stimulating hormone)

Gonadotrophs (luteinizing hormone and follicle-stimulating hormone)

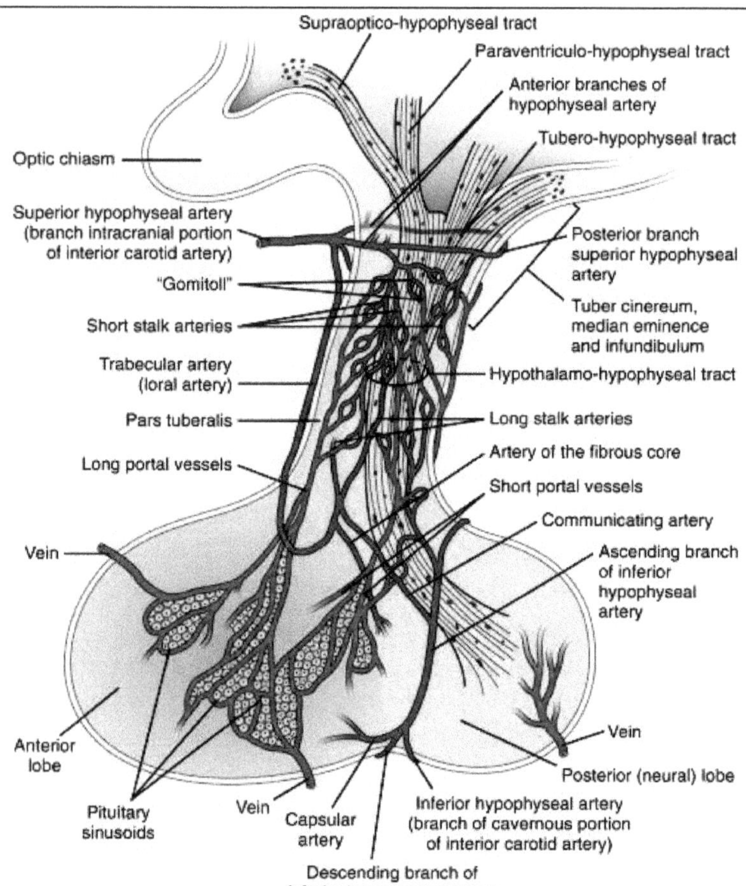

Anatomy of Pituitary Gland

Functions of the Pituitary Gland-

Each lobe of the pituitary gland produces certain hormones.

Anterior lobe:

- **Growth hormone**

- **Prolactin** - to stimulate milk production after

    Dr. Rajneesh Kumar Sharma

giving birth
- **ACTH (adrenocorticotropic hormone)** - to stimulate the adrenal glands
- **TSH (thyroid-stimulating hormone)** - to stimulate the thyroid gland
- **FSH (follicle-stimulating hormone)** - to stimulate the ovaries and testes
- **LH (luteinizing hormone)** - to stimulate the ovaries or testes

Intermediate lobe:
- **Melanocyte-stimulating hormone** - to control skin pigmentation

Posterior lobe:
- **ADH (antidiuretic hormone)** - to increase absorption of water into the blood by the kidneys
- **Oxytocin** - to contract the uterus during childbirth and stimulate milk production

The anterior pituitary can also synthesize numerous other nonclassical peptides, growth factors, cytokines, binding proteins and neurotransmitters that are important for paracrine and/or autocrine control of anterior pituitary secretion and/or cell proliferation under defined physiological conditions.

Relationship among Hypothalamic, Pituitary, Target Glands, and Feedback Hormones			
Hypothalamic Regulatory Hormone	**Pituitary Hormone**	**Target Gland**	**Feedback Hormone**
TRH	TSH	Thyroid gland	T4, T3
LH-RH	LH	Gonad	E2, T
LH-RH	FSH	Gonad	Inhibin, E2, T
GH-RH, SMS	GH	Multi-organs	IGF-1
PIF	Prolactin	Breast	?
CRH, ADH	ACTH	Adrenal	Cortisol

ACTH = Adrenocorticotropin hormone; ADH = Antidiuretic hormone; CRH = Corticotropin-releasing hormone; E2 = Estradiol; FSH = Follicle-stimulating hormone; GH = Growth hormone; GH-RH = Growth hormone-releasing hormone; IGF = Insulin-like growth factor; LH = Luteinizing hormone; LH-RH = Luteinizing hormone-releasing hormone; PIF = Prolactin release-inhibitory factor; SMS = Somatostatin; T = Testosterone; T4 = Thyroxine; TRH = Thyrotropin-releasing hormone; TSH = thyroid-stimulating hormone

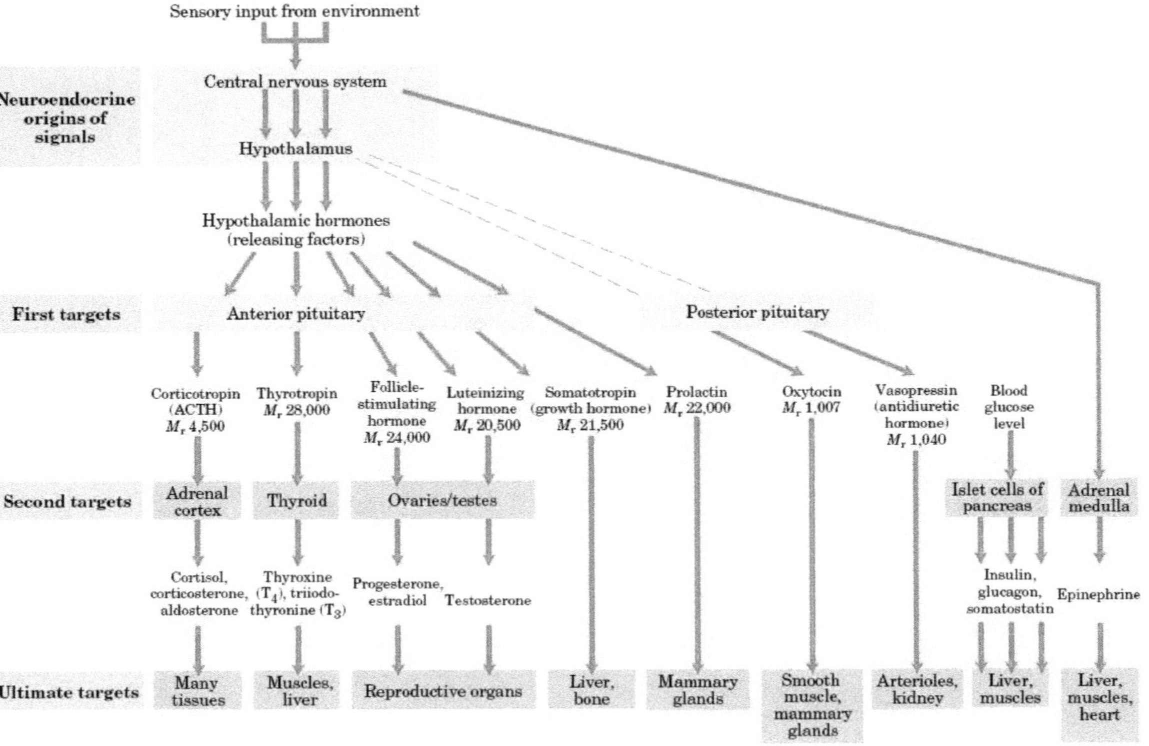

The major endocrine systems and their target tissues

Gross Anatomy

Location-

The hypothalamus lies directly above the pituitary gland and occupies approximately 2% of the brain volume.

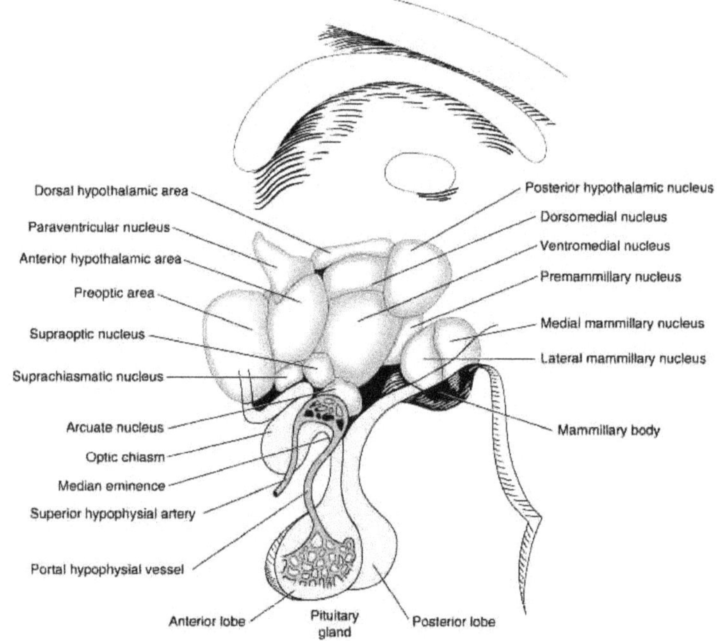

Anatomy and Relations of Hypothalamus

Appearance-

It is composed of a number of cell groups as well as fiber tracts that are symmetric about the third ventricle. The external surface of the hypothalamic floor gives rise to a median protuberance called the tuber cinereum, whose central part extends anteriorly and downward into a funnel-like process, the infundibulum or median

     Dr. Rajneesh Kumar Sharma

eminence. The infundibulum is in direct continuity with the infudibular stem of the posterior pituitary gland, and together with the pars tuberalis of the anterior pituitary, forms the pituitary stalk. Two additional symmetric eminences, the lateral eminences, corresponding to the most lateral portion of the hypothalamic wall and the postinfundibular eminence, as well as the symmetric mammillary bodies, complete the macroscopic morphology of the hypothalamic floor.

Hypothalamic Neurohypophysial Tract

The hypothalamic neurohypophysial tract defines the neuronal system terminating in the posterior pituitary and is best known for its secretion of vasopressin and oxytocin into the peripheral circulation to regulate water balance (antidiuresis), milk ejection and uterine contraction.

Hypothalamic Pituitary Axis

The hypothalamic-pituitary axis is composed of the hypothalamus, infundibular stalk, posterior pituitary, and anterior pituitary.

Functions of Hypothalamus

The general functions of the hypothalamus are of extreme importance for the body, such as-
1. Pituitary Gland Regulation
2. Blood Pressure Regulation
3. Hunger and Salt Cravings
4. Feeding Reflexes
5. Thirst
6. Body Temperature Regulation
7. Hydration

8. Heart Rate
9. Bladder Function
10. Water Preservation
11. Hormonal/Neurotransmitter Regulation
12. Ovarian Function
13. Testicular Function
14. Mood & Behavioral Functions
15. Wakefulness
16. Metabolism
17. Sleep Cycles
18. Energy Levels
19. Homoeostasis

The hypothalamus has many functions and is one of the major regulators of homeostasis.

- It controls the autonomic nervous system, acts with the limbic system to regulate emotional and behavioral patterns, regulates eating and drinking, controls body temperature and regulates diurnal rhythms. It also controls pituitary gland secretions.
- The hypothalamus receives input from the external and internal environment as well as having its own receptors. It receives stimuli from the somatic and visceral sense organs. These inputs travel via the medulla oblongata and reach the hypothalamus through innervations by fibers producing dopamine, adrenaline, noradrenaline, serotonin and acetylcholine as well as fibers releasing neuropeptides such as enkephalins, NPY, neurotensin, dynorphins and endorphins.
- The release of hormones from the pituitary is therefore subject to many different stimuli from 'higher centers' acting on the hypothalamus.

   Dr. Rajneesh Kumar Sharma

- In response to stimuli such as stress, pain and emotions, the hypothalamus can exert effects on the anterior and posterior pituitary gland in order to respond rapidly to environmental change as well as to feedback from internal systems.

Feedback Control

Feedback mechanisms, both negative and positive, are essential for regulating the function of the hypothalamic-pituitary-target organ axis.

1. **Negative Feedback**: This mechanism helps maintain hormonal balance. After hypothalamic hormones stimulate or inhibit pituitary hormone release, these pituitary hormones act on target glands (e.g., thyroid, adrenal glands), triggering the release of further hormones or metabolic effects. Hypothalamic hormone actions can be inhibited by:
   - Long feedback loops from hormones produced by target glands.
   - Short feedback loops from pituitary hormones.
   - Direct feedback from target gland hormones to the pituitary gland.
2. **Positive Feedback**: While less common, positive feedback also plays a role in specific physiological processes. For example:
   - In the menstrual cycle, high estradiol levels can trigger a surge in luteinizing hormone (LH) levels, leading to ovulation.

This positive feedback loop is crucial for regulating reproductive cycles.

These feedback mechanisms ensure hormone levels remain balanced by adjusting secretion based on internal and external factors. The hypothalamus integrates input from higher brain centers, integrating signals related to internal states, external stimuli, and emotional responses, influencing hormone release control.

In conclusion, feedback mechanisms involving negative and positive loops regulate the hypothalamic-pituitary-target organ axis, maintaining hormone balance and coordinating physiological functions crucial for overall health and homeostasis.

Hypothalamic Hormone Effects on the Anterior Pituitary Gland

- **Thyrotropin Releasing Hormone (TRH)**: Stimulates the release of Thyroid Stimulating Hormone (TSH) and Prolactin (PRL).
- **Gonadotropin Releasing Hormone (GnRH)**: Stimulates the release of Luteinizing Hormone (LH) and Follicle-Stimulating Hormone (FSH).
- **Growth Hormone Releasing Hormone (GHRH)**: Stimulates the release of Growth Hormone (GH).
- **Somatostatin (SS)**: Inhibits the release of Growth Hormone (GH).
- **Corticotropin Releasing Hormone (CRH)**: Stimulates the release of Adrenocorticotropic Hormone (ACTH).

- **Dopamine (DA)**: Inhibits the release of Prolactin (PRL).

These hypothalamic hormones play key roles in regulating the anterior pituitary gland's secretion of specific hormones, influencing various physiological processes such as metabolism, reproduction, growth, and stress response.

Hormones: A Brief Study

Definition of Hormones: The term "hormone" originates from a Greek phrase meaning "to set in motion." Hormones are chemical substances secreted by individual cells or groups of cells into body fluids, exerting physiological control over other cells within the body.

Types of Hormones:

Hormones can be categorized as follows:

1. **Local Hrmones:** These are released from nearby cells and affect specific local areas. For example, acetylcholine is released at parasympathetic and skeletal nerve endings, secretin from the duodenal wall, and cholecystokinin from the small intestine.
2. **General Hormones:** Secreted by specific endocrine glands, these hormones are transported through the bloodstream to exert physiological effects at distant points in the body. Examples include growth hormone and thyroid hormones.

Chemistry of Hormones:

Hormones can be classified based on their chemical composition:

1. **Proteins or Derivatives of Proteins:** Hormones from the pancreas and anterior pituitary are

proteins, those from the posterior pituitary are peptides, and those from the thyroid and adrenal medulla are amino acid derivatives.

2. **Steroid Hormones:** Derived from glands originating from the mesenchymal zone of the embryo, such as the adrenal cortex, ovary, and testes.

Major Classes of Hormones:

Hormones fall into five primary classes:

1. **Amino Acid Derivatives:** Examples include dopamine, catecholamines, and thyroid hormones.
2. **Small Neuropeptides:** Such as gonadotropin-releasing hormone (GnRH), thyrotropin-releasing hormone (TRH), somatostatin, and vasopressin.
3. **Large Proteins:** Insulin, luteinizing hormone (LH), and parathyroid hormone (PTH) are produced by classic endocrine glands.
4. **Steroid Hormones:** Examples include cortisol and estrogen, synthesized from cholesterol-based precursors.
5. **Vitamin Derivatives:** Such as retinoids and vitamin D.

Target Tissue:

Specific hormones affect particular organs or tissues known as target organs or tissues. For instance, adrenocorticotropic hormone (ACTH) from the anterior pituitary affects the adrenal cortex, while ovarian hormones primarily influence the reproductive organs.

Hormone Synthesis and Processing:

Peptide hormones and their receptors are synthesized through a classic pathway of gene expression:

Transcription → mRNA → Protein → Posttranslational Processing → Intracellular Sorting → Membrane Integration → Secretion

Steroid hormones, on the other hand, are synthesized from cholesterol through multiple regulated enzymatic steps.

Hormone Secretion, Transport, and Degradation:

The circulating level of a hormone is influenced by:

- Rate of secretion
- Circulating half-life

Peptide hormones (e.g., GnRH, insulin, GH) are stored in secretory granules and released upon stimulation, while steroid hormones diffuse directly into the circulation.

Control over Hormone Secretion:

Hormone secretion is controlled by negative feedback mechanisms, which prevent excessive secretion once the physiological effect is achieved. This feedback loop

 Dr. Rajneesh Kumar Sharma

involves signals that inhibit further hormone release when the desired effect is attained.

Amino Acids:

Amino acids are protein building blocks, with 20 different types used to synthesize proteins. Each amino acid contains an alpha carbon atom attached to a hydrogen atom, an amino group (-NH2), a carboxyl group (-COOH), and a unique "R" group that determines its properties.

Understanding the chemistry and regulation of hormones is crucial for comprehending their diverse physiological roles in maintaining homeostasis and overall health.

Amino Acid Characteristics and Abbreviations

Here is an presentation of amino acid characteristics and their abbreviations:

1. **Alanine (Ala, A):** Hydrophobic
2. **Arginine (Arg, R):** Basic and hydrophilic due to the free amino group
3. **Asparagine (Asn, N):** Can be covalently linked to carbohydrates ("N-linked") via its -NH group
4. **Aspartic Acid (Asp, D):** Acidic and hydrophilic due to the free carboxyl group
5. **Cysteine (Cys, C):** Oxidation of sulfhydryl (-SH) groups can link two cysteines (disulfide bond - S-S)

6. **Glutamic Acid (Glu, E):** Acidic and hydrophilic due to the free carboxyl group
7. **Glutamine (Gln, Q):** Moderately hydrophilic
8. **Glycine (Gly, G):** Very small and amphiphilic (can exist in various environments)
9. **Histidine (His, H):** Basic and hydrophilic
10. **Isoleucine (Ile, I):** Hydrophobic
11. **Leucine (Leu, L):** Hydrophobic
12. **Lysine (Lys, K):** Strongly basic and hydrophilic
13. **Methionine (Met, M):** Hydrophobic
14. **Phenylalanine (Phe, F):** Very hydrophobic
15. **Proline (Pro, P):** Causes kinks in the peptide chain due to its cyclic structure
16. **Serine (Ser, S):** Can be covalently linked to carbohydrates ("O-linked") via its -OH group
17. **Threonine (Thr, T):** Can be covalently linked to carbohydrates ("O-linked") via its -OH group
18. **Tryptophan (Trp, W):** Relatively rare in plant proteins
19. **Tyrosine (Tyr, Y):** Phosphate or sulfate groups can be covalently attached to its -OH group
20. **Valine (Val, V):** Hydrophobic

Understanding the properties and roles of these amino acids is fundamental to understanding protein structure, function, and interactions within biological systems. Each amino acid contributes uniquely to the structure and function of proteins.

Some Important Hormones: Structure and Functions

Pituitary Hormones

- **Oxytocin**
  - **Structure:** Polypeptide of 9 amino acids (CYIQNCPLG with disulfide bonds)
  - **Functions:** Stimulates uterine contraction, milk ejection in lactating females, responds to suckling reflex and estradiol, inhibits steroid synthesis in testes
- **Vasopressin (Antidiuretic Hormone, ADH)**
  - **Structure:** Polypeptide of 9 amino acids (CYFQNCPRG with disulfide bonds)
  - **Functions:** Regulates blood pressure, increases water reabsorption from distal tubules in kidneys in response to extracellular [Na+]
- **Melanocyte-Stimulating Hormones (MSH)**
  - **α-Polypeptide:** 13 amino acids
  - **β-Polypeptide:** 18 amino acids
  - **γ-Polypeptide:** 12 amino acids
  - **Functions:** Involved in pigmentation regulation
- **Corticotropin (Adrenocorticotropin, ACTH)**
  - **Structure:** Polypeptide of 39 amino acids
  - **Functions:** Stimulates adrenal gland cells to increase steroid synthesis and secretion
- **Lipotropin (LPH)**
  - **β-Polypeptide:** 93 amino acids
  - **γ-Polypeptide:** 60 amino acids
  - **Functions:** Increases fatty acid release from adipocytes

- **Thyrotropin (Thyroid-Stimulating Hormone, TSH)**
  - α-**Polypeptide:** 96 amino acids
  - β-**Polypeptide:** 112 amino acids
  - **Functions:** Stimulates thyroid follicle cells to synthesize thyroid hormones
- **Growth Hormone (GH or Somatotropin)**
  - **Structure:** Protein of 191 amino acids
  - **Functions:** General anabolic stimulant, increases insulin-like growth factor-I (IGF-I), promotes cell growth and bone growth
- **Prolactin (PRL)**
  - **Structure:** Protein of 197 amino acids
  - **Functions:** Stimulates mammary gland cell differentiation and milk synthesis
- **Luteinizing Hormone (LH) / Human Chorionic Gonadotropin (hCG)**
  - α-**Polypeptide:** 96 amino acids
  - β-**Polypeptide:** 121 amino acids
  - **Functions:** Increases progesterone synthesis in ovaries, stimulates testosterone synthesis in testes, and promotes interstitial cell development
- **Follicle-Stimulating Hormone (FSH)**
  - α-**Polypeptide:** 96 amino acids
  - β-**Polypeptide:** 120 amino acids
  - **Functions:** Stimulates ovarian follicle development, ovulation, estrogen production, and spermatogenesis

Hypothalamic Hormones

- **Corticotropin-Releasing Factor (CRF or CRH)**
  - **Structure:** Polypeptide of 41 amino acids
  - **Functions:** Stimulates corticotrope cells to release ACTH and β-endorphin (Lipotropin)
- **Gonadotropin-Releasing Factor (GnRF or GnRH)**
  - **Structure:** Polypeptide of 10 amino acids
  - **Functions:** Stimulates gonadotrope cells to release LH and FSH
- **Prolactin-Releasing Factor (PRF) / Prolactin-Release Inhibiting Factor (PIF)**
  - **Functions:** Stimulates or inhibits prolactin release from lactotrope cells
- **Growth Hormone-Releasing Factor (GRF or GRH)**
  - **Structure:** Polypeptide of 40 and 44 amino acids
  - **Functions:** Stimulates growth hormone (GH) secretion
- **Somatostatin (SIF or Growth Hormone-Release Inhibiting Factor, GIF)**
  - **Structure:** Polypeptide of 14 and 28 amino acids
  - **Functions:** Inhibits GH and TSH secretion
- **Thyrotropin-Releasing Factor (TRH or TRF)**
  - **Structure:** Polypeptide of 3 amino acids (EHP)
  - **Functions:** Stimulates TSH and prolactin secretion

Thyroid Hormones

- **Thyroxine and Triiodothyronine**
  - **Structure:** Iodinated dityrosine derivatives
  - **Functions:** Stimulate oxidation in various cells in response to TSH
- **Calcitonin**
  - **Structure:** Protein of 32 amino acids
  - **Functions:** Regulates calcium and phosphate metabolism

Gut Hormones

- **Glucagon-like Peptide 1 (GLP-1)**
  - **Structure:** 31 or 30 amino acids
  - **Functions:** Enhances glucose-dependent insulin secretion, inhibits glucagon secretion and gastric emptying
- **Glucose-Dependent Insulinotropic Polypeptide (GIP)**
  - **Structure:** Polypeptide of 42 amino acids
  - **Functions:** Inhibits gastric acid secretion, enhances insulin secretion
- **Ghrelin**
  - **Structure:** 28 amino acids
  - **Functions:** Stimulates appetite, regulates energy homeostasis, glucose metabolism, and gastric secretion
- **Gastrin**
  - **Structure:** 17 amino acids
  - **Functions:** Stimulates acid and pepsin secretion, pancreatic secretions

- **Secretin**
  - **Structure:** 27 amino acids
  - **Functions:** Stimulates pancreatic bicarbonate and water secretion
- **Cholecystokinin (CCK)**
  - **Structure:** 33 amino acids
  - **Functions:** Stimulates gallbladder contraction, bile flow, and pancreatic enzyme secretion

Pancreatic Hormones

- **Insulin**
  - **Structure:** Disulfide-bonded dipeptide of 21 and 30 amino acids
  - **Functions:** Increases glucose uptake/utilization, promotes lipogenesis and anabolism
- **Glucagon**
  - **Structure:** Polypeptide of 29 amino acids
  - **Functions:** Increases lipid mobilization and glycogenolysis to raise blood glucose levels
- **Pancreatic Polypeptide (PP)**
  - **Structure:** Polypeptide of 36 amino acids
  - **Functions:** Increases glycogenolysis, regulates gastrointestinal activity
- **Somatostatin**
  - **Structure:** 14 amino acid version
  - **Functions:** Inhibits glucagon and somatotropin release

Placental Hormones

- **Estrogens**
    - **Type:** Steroids (e.g., estradiol, estrone)
    - **Function:** Essential for maintaining pregnancy and the maturation/function of female secondary sex organs
- **Progestins**
    - **Type:** Steroid (e.g., progesterone)
    - **Function:** Mimics the actions of progesterone, crucial for implantation of the ovum and maintenance of pregnancy
- **Chorionic Gonadotropin**
    - **Structure:** Two proteins: α (96 amino acids) and β (147 amino acids)
    - **Function:** Exhibits activity similar to luteinizing hormone (LH), supporting ovarian function during pregnancy
- **Placental Lactogen**
    - **Structure:** Protein of 191 amino acids
    - **Function:** Acts similarly to prolactin and growth hormone, contributing to lactation and metabolic regulation during pregnancy
- **Relaxin**
    - **Structure:** Two proteins of 22 and 32 amino acids
    - **Function:** Inhibits myometrial contractions, supporting relaxation of pelvic ligaments during gestation

Gonadal Hormones

- **Estrogens (Ovarian)**
    - **Type:** Steroids (e.g., estradiol, estrone)
    - **Function:** Promotes maturation and function of female secondary sex organs
- **Progestins (Ovarian)**
    - **Type:** Steroid (e.g., progesterone)
    - **Function:** Facilitates implantation of the ovum and maintenance of pregnancy
- **Androgens (Testicular)**
    - **Type:** Steroid (e.g., testosterone)
    - **Function:** Essential for the maturation and function of male secondary sex organs
- **Inhibins A and B**
    - **Structure:** α subunit (134 amino acids); β subunit (115 and 116 amino acids)
    - **Function:** Inhibits follicle-stimulating hormone (FSH) secretion, regulating reproductive processes

Adrenal Cortical Hormones

- **Glucocorticoids**
    - **Type:** Steroids (e.g., cortisol, corticosterone)
    - **Function:** Diverse effects on inflammation and protein synthesis
- **Mineralocorticoids**
    - **Type:** Steroids (e.g., aldosterone)
    - **Function:** Maintains electrolyte and fluid balance, particularly sodium and potassium levels

Adrenal Medullary Hormones

- **Epinephrine (Adrenalin)**
  - **Source:** Derived from tyrosine
  - **Function:** Stimulates glycogenolysis, lipid mobilization, smooth muscle contraction, and cardiac function
- **Norepinephrine (Noradrenalin)**
  - **Source:** Derived from tyrosine
  - **Function:** Promotes lipid mobilization and arteriole contraction

Liver Hormones

- **Angiotensin II**
  - **Structure:** Polypeptide of 8 amino acids
  - **Function:** Induces essential hypertension by stimulating aldosterone synthesis and release

Kidney Hormones

- **Calcitriol (1,25-(OH)2-Vitamin D3)**
  - **Source:** Derived from 7-dehydrocholesterol
  - **Function:** Maintains calcium and phosphorus homeostasis, enhances intestinal calcium absorption, and regulates bone mineralization

Cardiac Hormones

- **Atrial Natriuretic Peptide (ANP)**
    - **Source:** Released from heart atria in response to hypovolemia
    - **Function:** Acts on adrenal cells to reduce aldosterone production and promotes smooth muscle relaxation

Pineal Hormones

- **Melatonin**
    - **Source:** N-acetyl-5-methoxytryptamine
    - **Function:** Regulates circadian rhythms and sleep-wake cycles

This overview provides concise details about various hormones, their structures, and important functions in the body. Each hormone plays a critical role in maintaining physiological balance and supporting reproductive, metabolic, and regulatory processes essential for overall health and well-being.

Definition

The breast is a compound alveolar gland, characteristic of mammals, composed of 15 to 20 lobes of glandular tissue separated by interlobular septa. Each lobe is drained by a lactiferous duct that opens at the nipple. The breast functions for nourishment through milk secretion and serves as a secondary sexual feature in females. It is one of two hemispheric projections of variable size located in the subcutaneous layer overlying the pectoralis major muscle on each side of the mature female chest, and it is rudimentary in males. Synonyms: mamma, mammary gland, teat, nipple, breast, papilla.

Embryology of the Breast

Sebaceous glands, sweat glands, and mammary glands all originate from epidermal proliferations. Developmentally, mammary glands are derived from modified sweat glands.

In females, significant growth and differentiation of breast tissues occur after puberty, leading to the development of a complex structure. The initial indication of mammary glands begins with a band-like thickening of the epidermis known as the mammary line or mammary ridge.

          Dr. Rajneesh Kumar Sharma

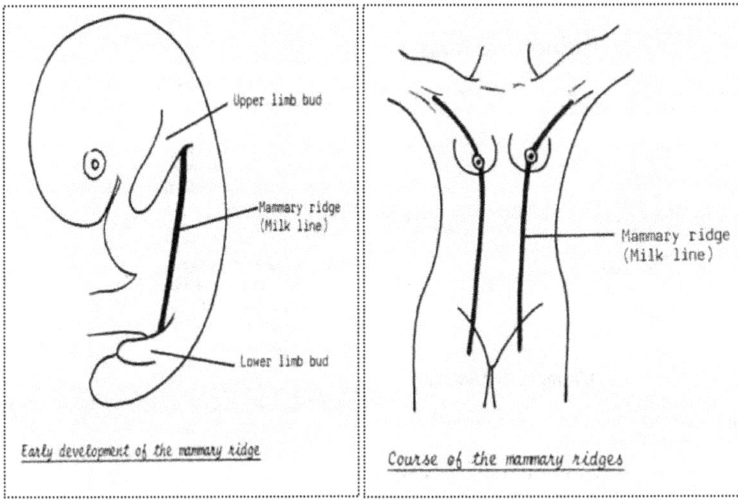

Skin appendages arising from mammary ridge (Milk line) — Ectoderm

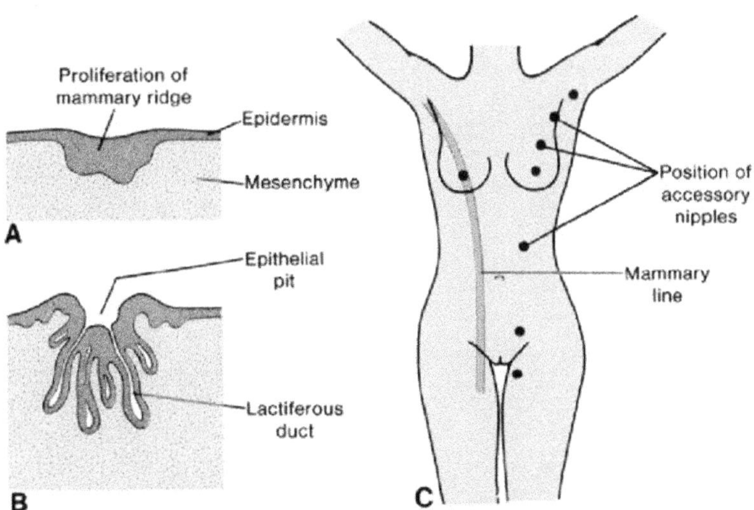

A-B- Sections through the developing mammary gland at the third and eighth months, respectively. C- Positions of accessory nipples (Blue line- mammary line)

Formation of Mammary Line (7-Week Embryo)

During embryonic development at 7 weeks, the mammary line extends bilaterally from the base of the forelimb to the region of the hindlimb.

Persistence and Sprouting of Mammary Line

While most of the mammary line regresses, a small portion in the thoracic region persists and penetrates the underlying mesenchyme, giving rise to 16 to 24 sprouts.

Development of Mammary Buds

These sprouts develop into small, solid buds as the embryo matures.

Canalization and Differentiation

By the end of prenatal life, the epithelial sprouts become canalized, forming the lactiferous ducts, and the buds develop into small ducts and alveoli of the gland.

Postnatal Nipple Formation

Shortly after birth, the small epithelial pit where lactiferous ducts open transforms into the nipple due to mesenchymal proliferation.

Structure of Young Adult Female Breast

Anatomical Features

Each breast in a young adult female is a rounded eminence situated within the superficial fascia, primarily anterior to the upper thorax and spreading laterally.

Nipple and Areola

The breast is characterized by a centrally located nipple on its anterior aspect, surrounded by the areola.

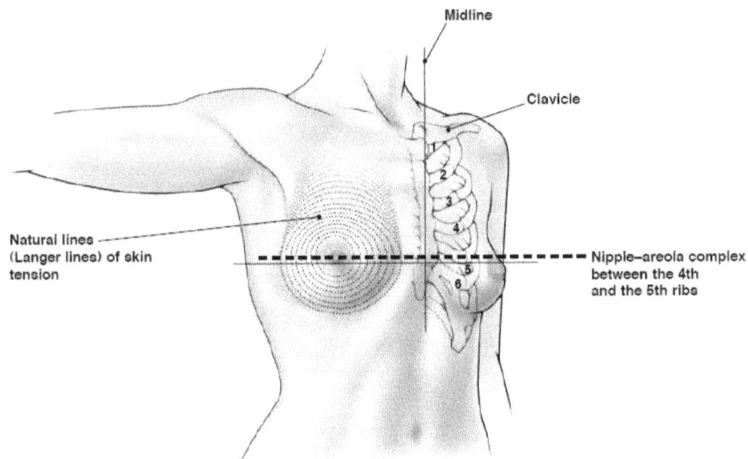

Surface Anatomy of the Breast

Development Along the Milk Line

Origin and Pathway

The breasts develop along the milk line or mammary ridge, a band-like thickening of ectoderm extending from just below the axilla to the inguinal region bilaterally.

Embryonic Primordia

In human embryos, mammary glands originate from primordia in the thoracic part of the milk line, guiding the subsequent development of the breasts.

In the adult female, the breast occupies an area extending vertically from the second or third to the sixth rib and transversely from the sternal edge medially to almost the midaxillary line laterally. It is anatomically divided into four main parts:

1. Upper Inner Quadrant (Superomedial)- Located in the superomedial region of the breast.

2. Lower Inner Quadrant (Inferomedial)- Situated in the inferomedial aspect of the breast.

3. Upper Outer Quadrant (Superolateral)- Found in the superolateral area of the breast.

4. Lower Outer Quadrant (Inferolateral)- Located in the inferolateral part of the breast.

Tail of Spence

The tail of Spence represents the extension of the breast tissue into the axilla along the inferolateral edge of the pectoralis major muscle. It projects slightly beyond the main breast mass and may extend through the deep fascia up to the apex of the axilla, commonly referred to as the axillary tail of Spence. This region is significant in breast examination and pathology.

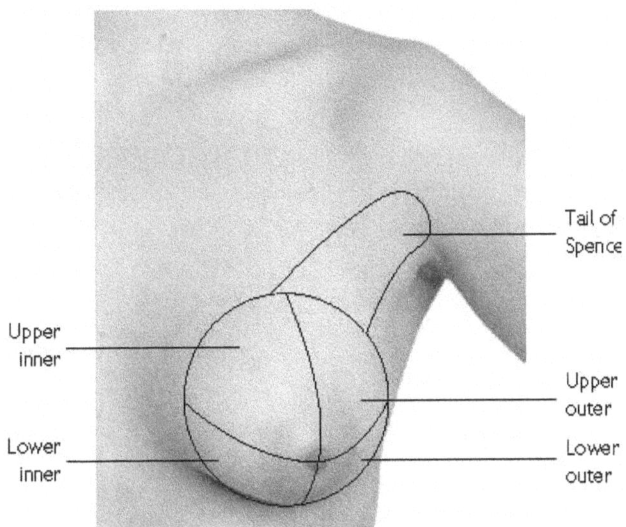

Anatomical Quadrants of Breast

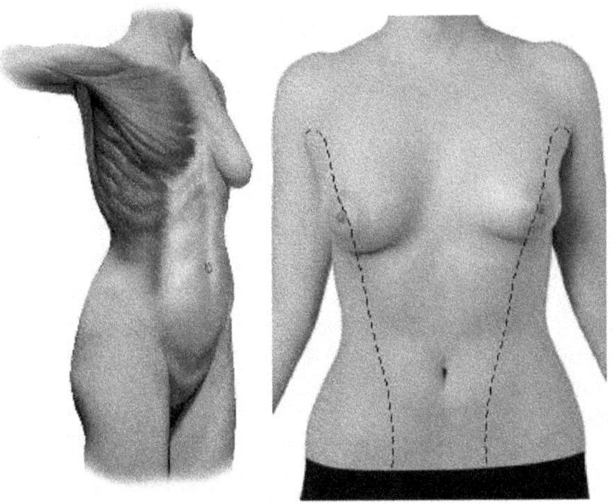

Position of the Breast and Milk Lines

Anatomical relations of breast-

The breast lies upon the deep pectoral fascia, which in turn overlies pectoralis major and serratus anterior, and below, obliquus externus abdominis and its aponeurosis as that forms the anterior wall of the sheath of rectus abdominis. Between the breast and the deep fascia is loose connective tissue in the retromammary (submammary) 'space', which allows the breast some degree of movement on the deep pectoral fascia. Occasionally, small projections of glandular tissue may pass through the deep fascia into the underlying muscle in normal subjects.

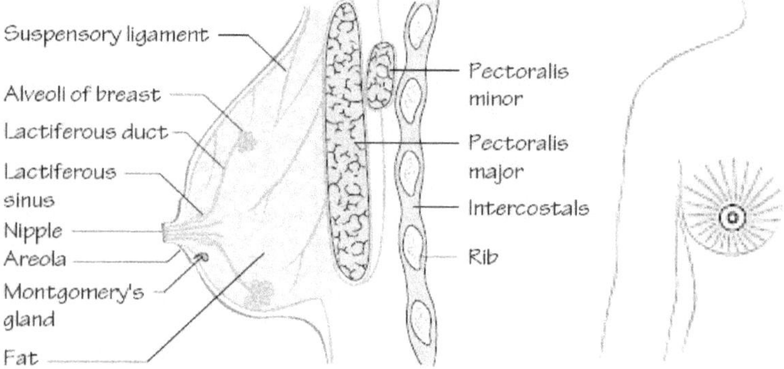

Anatomic Relations of the Breast and Arrangement of Lactiferous Ducts

Breast Shape and Size

The orb-like shape of breasts serves a physiological function by aiding in heat retention, which is essential for milk production.

 Dr. Rajneesh Kumar Sharma

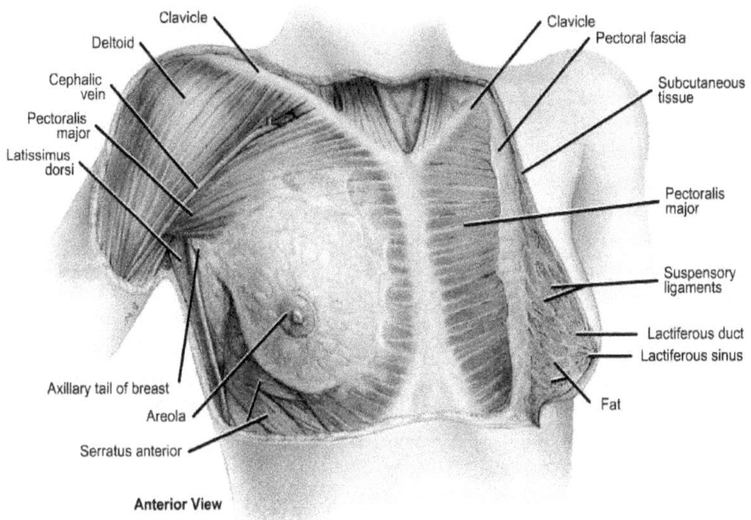

Anatomy of Breast

The shape of the human breast has likely evolved to prevent infants from suffocating while feeding. As human infants lack a protruding jaw like our evolutionary ancestors and other primates, a flat female chest could potentially block the infant's nose during feeding. This theory suggests that as the human jaw receded, breasts became larger to compensate for this anatomical change.

The size and shape of women's breasts vary significantly due to genetic, racial, and dietary factors, as well as age, parity (number of pregnancies carried to viability), and menopausal status. Breast shape can be hemispherical, conical, variably pendulous, piriform, or thin and flattened.

Factors Influencing Breast Size

Several factors influence a woman's breast size and shape:

- **Volume of Breast Tissue**: The amount of glandular and fat tissue in the breast.
- **Family History**: Genetic predisposition to breast size.
- **Age**: Breasts change in size and shape with age.
- **Weight Changes**: Significant weight loss or gain can affect breast size.
- **Pregnancy and Lactation History**: Changes due to pregnancies and breastfeeding.
- **Skin Thickness and Elasticity**: Influences how breasts change over time.
- **Hormonal Influences**: Particularly estrogen and progesterone levels.
- **Menopause**: Hormonal changes during menopause can affect breast size.

Internal Organization of the Breast

The breast is composed of:

- **Epithelial Glandular Tissue**: Arranged in 15–20 lobes, each connected to a lactiferous duct that converges at the nipple.
- **Fibrous Connective Tissue (Stroma)**: Surrounds and supports the glandular tissue.
- **Interlobar Adipose Tissue**: Fat tissue located between lobes.

- **Epithelial Secretory Tissue:** The lobes contain tubulo-alveolar epithelial glandular tissue that leads to lactiferous ducts.
- **Connective Tissue (Stroma):** The fibrous stroma surrounds and encloses the lobules, providing structural support. Fibrous condensations of stromal tissue extend from the ducts to the dermis, forming suspensory ligaments (Ligaments of Cooper) that help support breast tissue. These ligaments are particularly well-developed in the upper part of the breast.

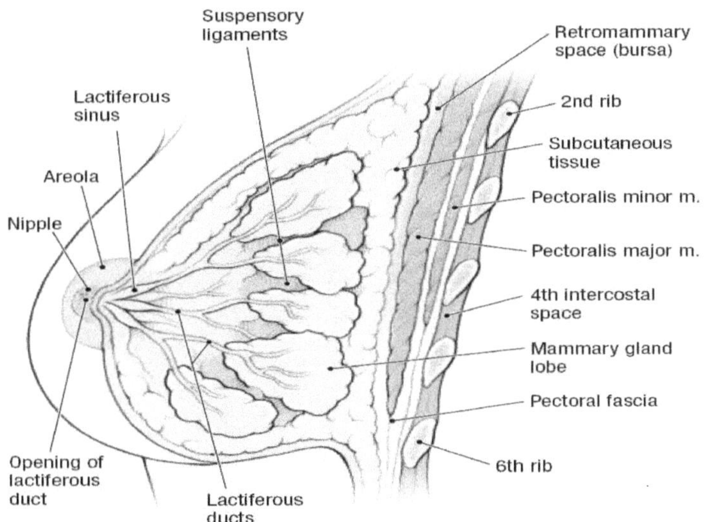

Breast in Saggittal Section

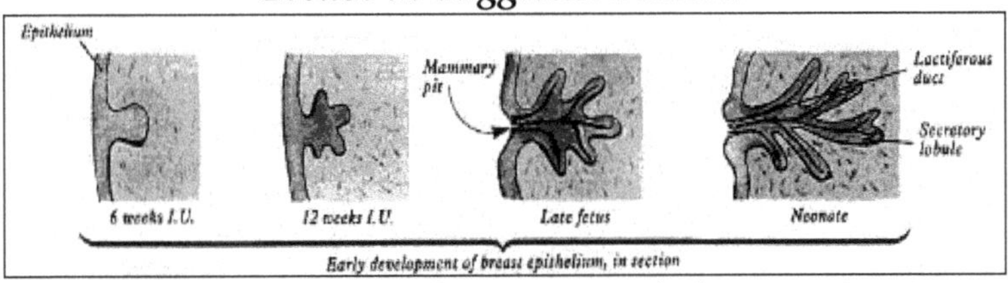

Early Development of Breast Epithelium in Section

Glandular Tissue

The mammary gland consists of branching ducts and terminal secretary lobules. These ducts converge into 15–20 larger lactiferous ducts that open at the apex of the nipple. Each lactiferous duct is connected to a tree-like system of ducts and lobules enclosed within connective tissue stroma, collectively forming a lobe of the mammary gland. The number of lobes corresponds to the number of lactiferous ducts.

Lobules are the secretory portions of the glands and their structure varies based on hormonal status. In the mature breast, each lobule comprises several blind-ending branches or expansions called alveoli or acini, which converge on an alveolar duct. These alveoli or acini are the sites of milk secretion.

Breast cancers typically arise at the junction of the lobules and ducts. As these cancers grow, they lead to the formation of fibrous tissue, resulting in hard and irregular masses.

Adipose tissue-

It surrounds the secretary tissue. It is highly variable in amount and is typically present in the interlobar stroma, and Blood vessels-

1- Arteries

Branches of the axillary artery, the internal thoracic artery, and some intercostal arteries, supply the female breast.

not amongst the lobules.

 Dr. Rajneesh Kumar Sharma

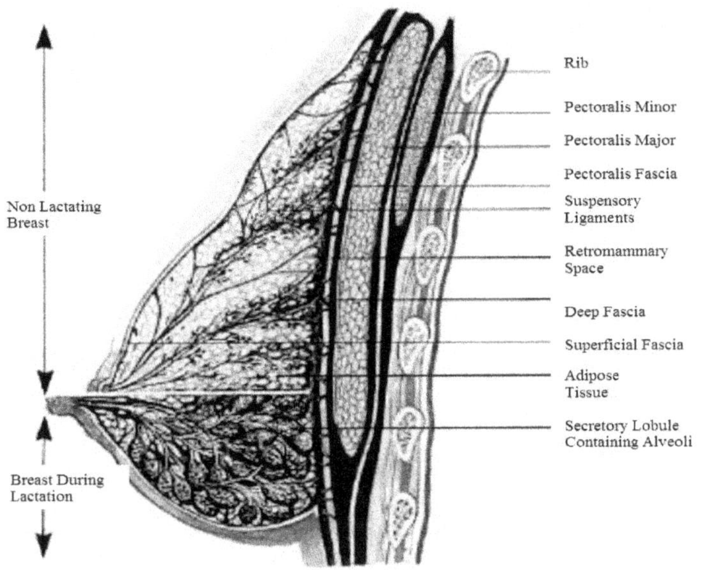

Comparative Anatomy of Nonlactating and Lactating Breast

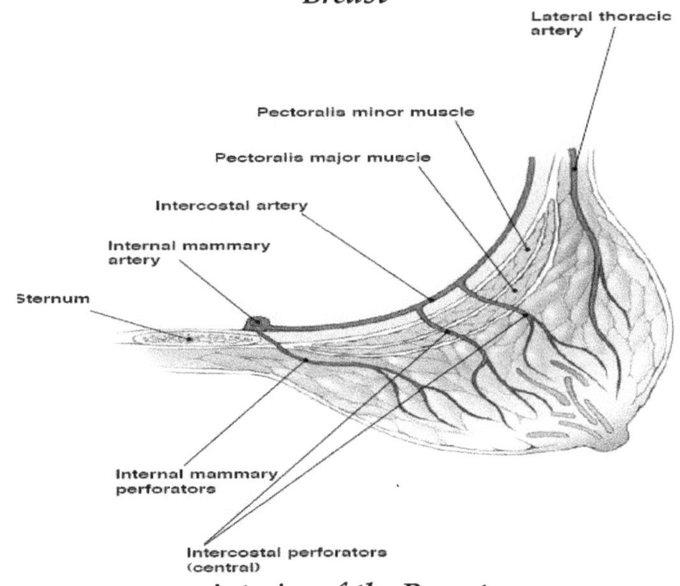

Arteries of the Breast

Axillary artery-

It supplies blood to the breast via several branches: the supreme thoracic, the pectoral branches of the thoraco-acromial artery, the lateral thoracic and the subscapular artery.

Internal thoracic artery-

It gives perforating branches to the anteromedial part of the breast.

Second to fourth intercostal arteries-

These give perforating branches more laterally in the anterior thorax. The second perforating artery is usually the largest, supplying the upper region of the breast, nipple, areola and adjacent breast tissue.

2- Veins

Around the areola there is a circular venous plexus. From areola and from the glandular tissue, blood drains in veins accompanying the arterial blood supply, i.e. to the axillary, internal thoracic and intercostal veins. Great individual variation may occur, and the axillary vein may be bifid.

Lymph Vessels

The lymphatic drainage of the breast can be very variable.

From the subareolar plexus, also known as Plexus of Sappey, there are efferent vessels draining to the following:

- The contralateral breast
- The internal mammary lymph node chain
- The mediastinal lymph nodes to the para-aortic lymph nodes, bronchomediastinal trunks, thoracic duct and right thoracic duct
- Inferiorly, the superior and inferior epigastric

lymphatic routes to the groin
- The axillary lymph nodes, the predominant site of drainage from the breast.

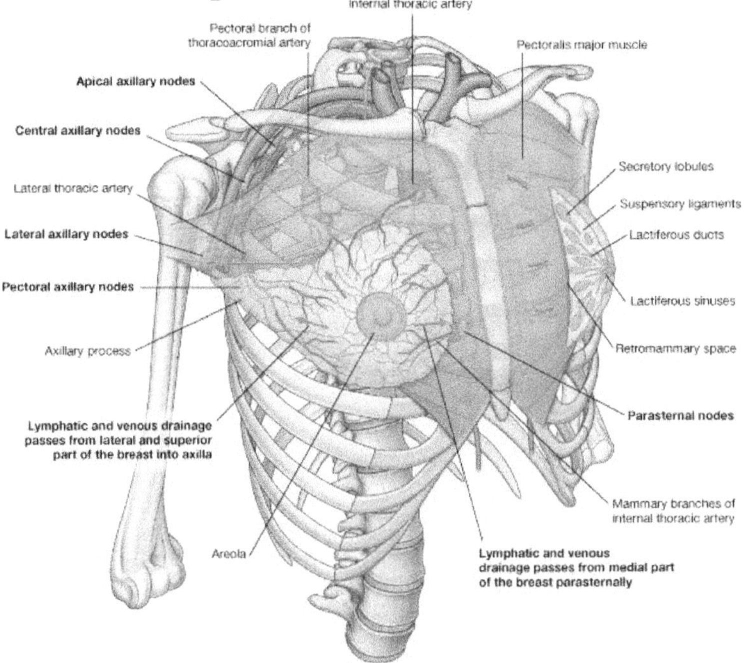

© Elsevier. Drake et al: Gray's Anatomy for Students - www.studentconsult.com

The Vasculature and Lymphatics of Breast

These lymph nodes number from 20–40; in the past these were named and grouped artificially as lower, central, subscapular, lateral and apical. According to modern nomenclature, based on the relation of the nodes to pectoralis minor the lymph nodes may be-
- **Level 1 or Low Nodes-** Those lying below Pectoralis Minor.
- **Level 2 or Middle Group Nodes-** Those behind the muscle.

- **Level 3 or Upper or Apical Nodes-** The nodes between the upper border of Pectoralis Minor and the lower border of the clavicle.
- **Rotter's nodes-** Between Pectoralis Minor and major there may be one or two other nodes.

The supratrochlear and deltopectoral nodes receive many superficial lymphatic vessels. The axillary nodes are indicated by capital letters.

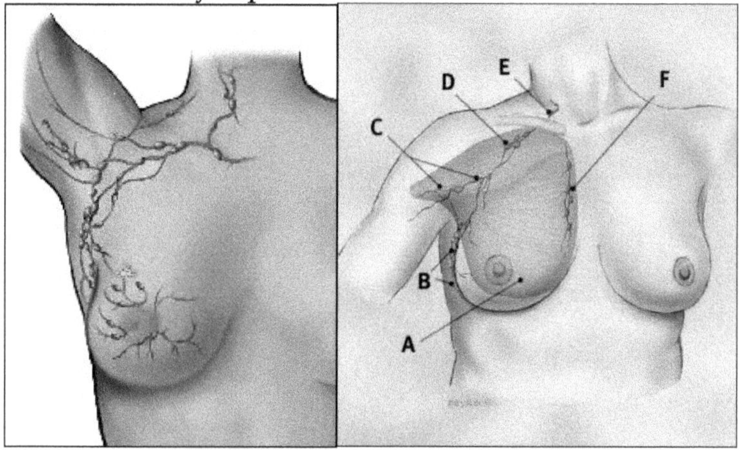

The Lymphatic System-Lymph node areas adjacent to breast area

(A- Pectoralis Major muscle, B- Axillary lymph nodes levels I, C- Axillary lymph nodes: levels II, D- Axillary lymph nodes levels III, E- Supraclavicular lymph nodes, F- Internal mammary lymph nodes)

The lateral nodes drain the upper limb. The subareolar plexus drains by collecting trunks into the axillary nodes. The pectoral nodes drain most of the breast. The apical nodes receive the lymph from the other axillary groups. Retropectoral ® and transpectoral (T) routes are also shown.

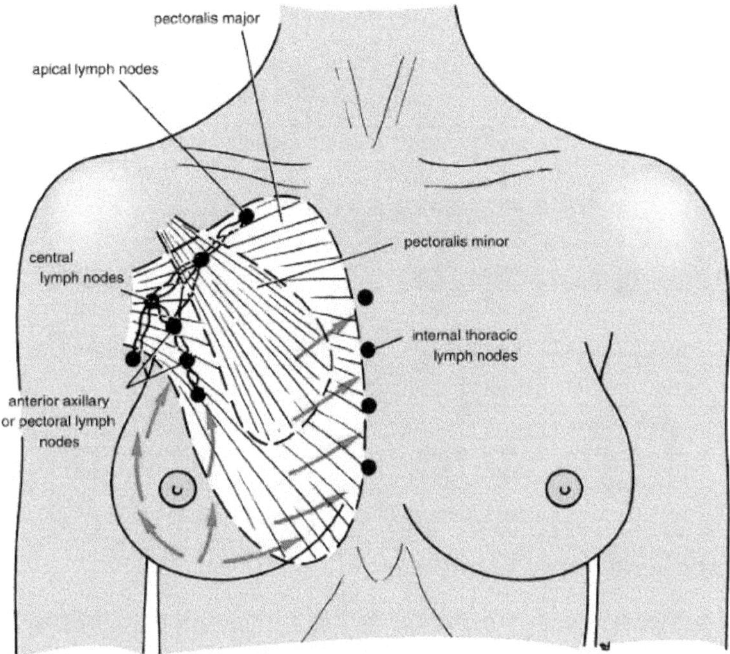

Diagram of the lymphatic drainage of the upper limb and breast

Nerves

The nerve supply of the breast is derived from the anterior and lateral branches of the fourth to sixth intercostal nerves which carry sensory and sympathetic efferent fibres.

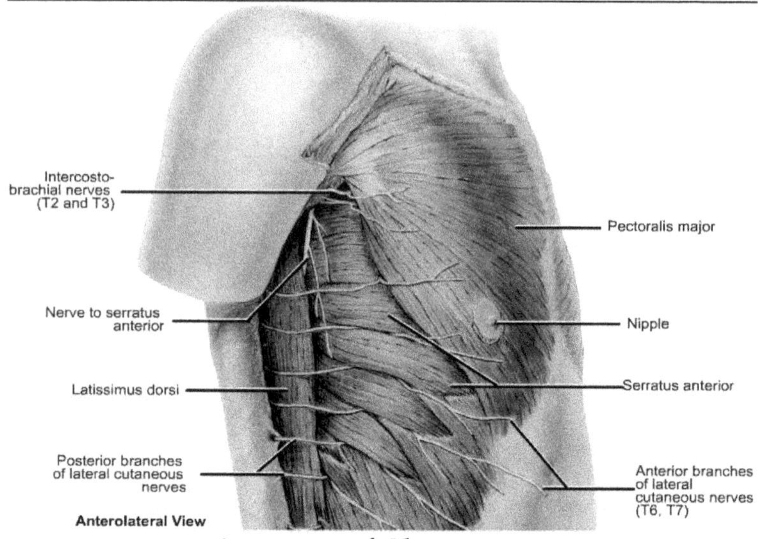

Anatomy of Chest Nerves

Nipple- Areolar Complex-

This complex is composed of the nipple located in the center of the areola.

Nipple

Synonyms-

Mammary- Papilla. Teat, Breast- Papilla.

Location of Nipple-

The nipple projects centrally from the anterior aspect. Its level in the thorax varies widely but is at the fourth intercostal space in most young women.

Nipple Shape and Size-

Its shape varies from conical to flattened, depending on nervous, hormonal, developmental and other factors. in the nulliparous it is pink or light brown or darker, depending on the general melanization of the body. It is covered by hairless skin; the epidermis has a deeply folded base interdigitating with dermal papillae, and scattered sebaceous glands open on to its surface. Melanocytes are quite numerous, giving the skin of the nipple a darker hue.

Anatomy of Nipple-

Internally the nipple is composed mostly of collagenous dense connective tissue with numerous elastic fibres which also spread beneath the areola, wrinkling the overlying skin. Smooth muscle cells are also present in and just deep to the nipple, disposed in a predominantly circular direction and radiating out from its base into the surrounding breast. Contraction of these smooth muscle cells, induced by cold or tactile (e.g. in suckling), or emotional stimuli causes erection of the nipple and wrinkling of the surrounding areola.

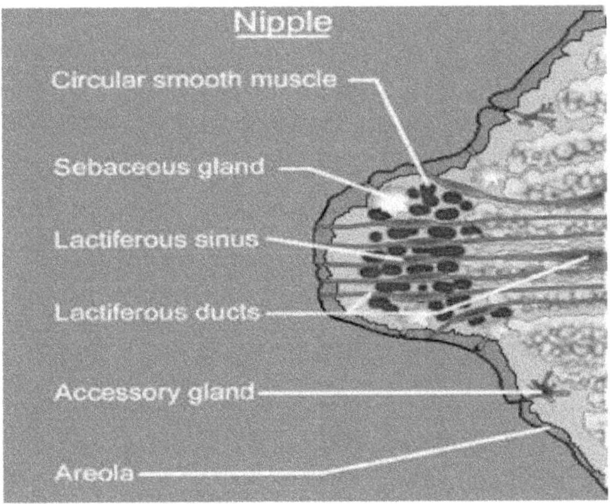

Section of Nipple

The lactiferous ducts traverse the nipple, their 15–20 minute orifices opening on to its wrinkled tip. Near its opening at the nipple each of these ducts is slightly expanded as a lactiferous sinus in the lactating breast by the presence of milk. Occasionally the nipple may not evert during prenatal development, remaining permanently retracted and so causing difficulty in suckling.

Areola

It is a discoid area of skin which encircles the base of the nipple.

Shape and size of Areola-

Its colour also varies from pink to dark brown depending on parity and race. Darkening of the nipple and areola occurs during the second month of pregnancy, and although it becomes a little paler after parturition, the change of hue is permanent.

Anatomy of Areola-

The nipple and especially the areola contains many sebaceous glands much enlarged in pregnancy and lactation as subcutaneous 'tubercles', whose oily secretion is a protective lubricant during lactation.

Glands of Montgomery

These are intermediate in structure between lactiferous and sweat glands; when visible to the naked eye they are creamy in colour. At the perimeter of the areola are large sudorific and sebaceous glands, the latter not accompanied by hairs. There is no adipose tissue immediately beneath the skin of the areola and papilla.

 Dr. Rajneesh Kumar Sharma

Breast Development

The breast development can be studied in follwing parts-

- Prenatal development
- Postnatal development
- Development during Pregnancy

Prenatal Development

Prenatal development is similar in both sexes, with the epithelial mammary bud appearing at a gestational age of 35 days. By day 37 this has become a mammary line extending from the axilla through to the inguinal region. Nipple formation begins at day 56 and primitive ducts or mammary sprouts develop at 84 days with canalization occurring at about the 150th day.

Abnormal Breast Conditions

During embryological development, due to certain causes, agenesis or malformation of the breast and its associated structures. These conditions may be due to genetic causes, various stimuli affecting organogenesis or mutations.

- **Amastia**: Absence of breast development in either sex, either unilaterally (on one side) or bilaterally (on both sides).
- **Amazia**: Presence of nipple development but absence of breast tissue.
- **Micromastia**: Postpubertal underdevelopment of breast tissue in women, leading to smaller breast size or hypoplasia.

- **Macromastia**: Postpubertal overdevelopment of breast tissue in women, resulting in larger breast size or hyperplasia.
- **Polymastia**: Presence of more than two breasts, a rare condition.
- **Athelia**: Rare condition where the nipple fails to develop.
- **Polythelia**: Development of multiple nipples, either within the mammary area or elsewhere (extramammary).
- **Poland Syndrome**: A rare birth defect characterized by underdevelopment or absence of the chest muscle (pectoralis) on one side of the body, often accompanied by webbing of the fingers (cutaneous syndactyly) on the same side (ipsilateral hand).
- **Inverted Nipple**: A condition where the lactiferous ducts open into the original epithelial pit, causing the nipple to retract or invert.

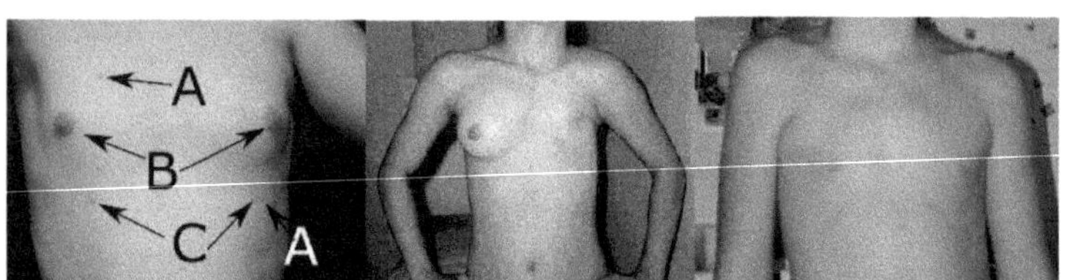

Supernumerary Accessory Nipples, Unilateral Amastia and Poland Syndrome

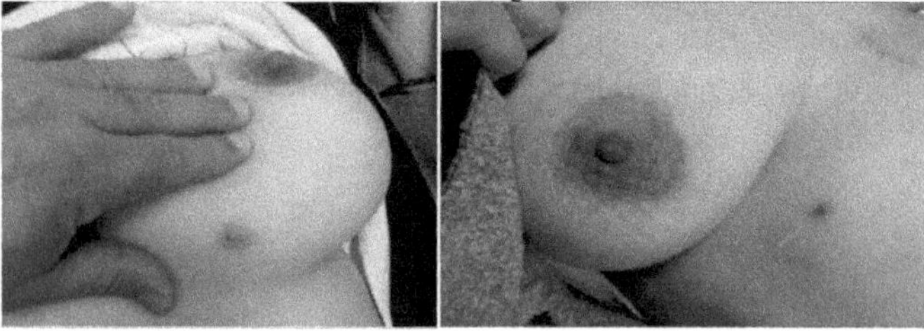

Dr. Rajneesh Kumar Sharma

Accessory Intra-mammary and Extra-mammary nipple

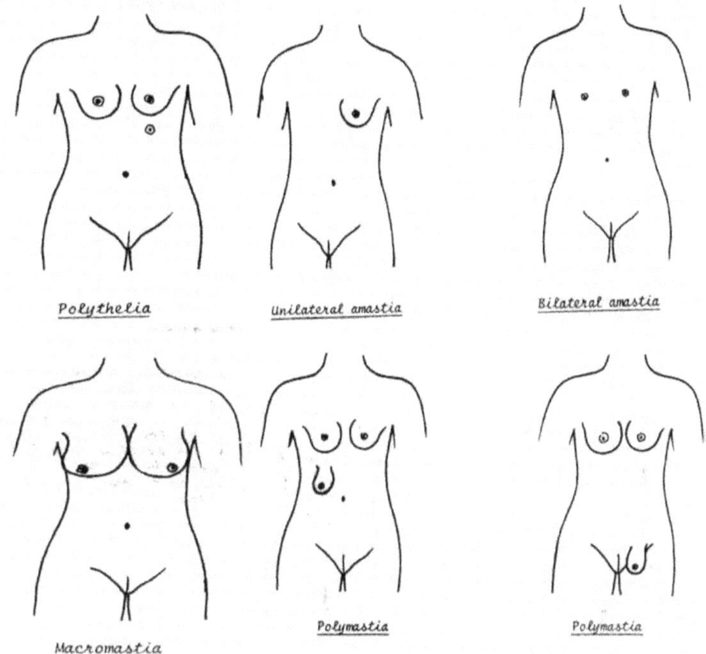

Some Conditions of abnormal Breast Development

Witch's Milk-

At birth the combination of fetal Prolactin and maternal oestrogen may give rise to transient hyperplasia and secretion of milk from the infant's mamma called as 'witch's milk'.

Postnatal Development

Lobule formation occurs, exclusively in females after puberty, when there is branching of ducts and development of lobules from terminal ducts. Externally recognizable breast development is called thelarche.

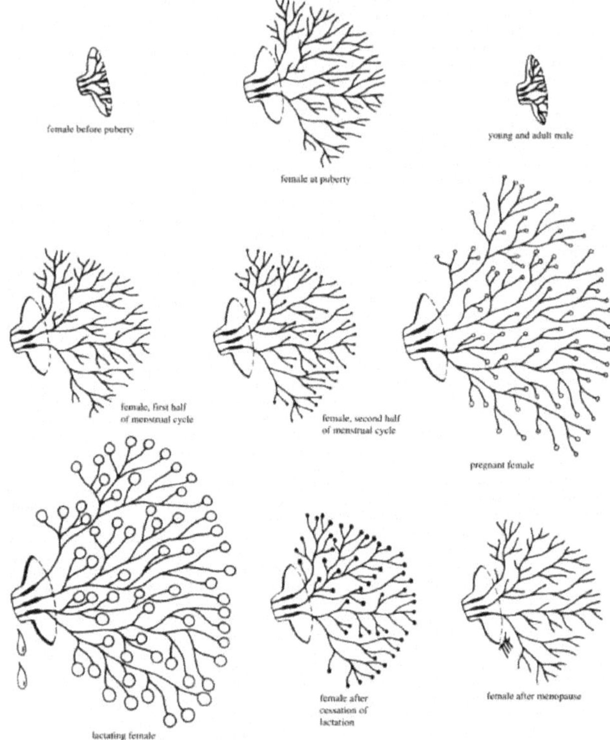

Ductal Development in Breasts of Male and Female

From puberty onwards the development of breast can be divided into five separate phases.

- **Phase I-** elevation of the nipple.
- **Phase II-** glandular subareolar tissue is present in both nipple and breast projecting from the chest wall as a single mass.
- **Phase III-** increase in diameter and pigmentation of the areola, with proliferation of palpable breast tissue.
- **Phase IV-** phase III progresses further, so that the

Dr. Rajneesh Kumar Sharma

nipple and areola form a secondary mass anterior to the main part of the breast now termed as areolo-nipple complex.

- **Phase V-** development of a smooth contour of the breast.

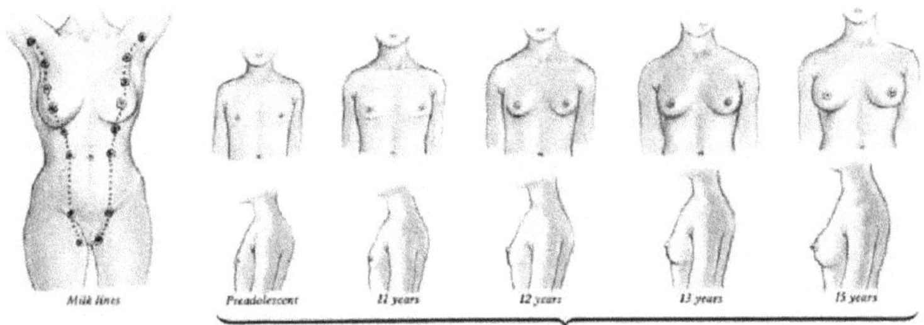

Before puberty	Early puberty	Late puberty
The breast is flat except for the nipple that sticks out from the chest.	The areola becomes a prominent bud; breasts begin to fill out.	Glandular tissue and fat increase in the breast, and areola becomes flat.

Development of Breast

During pregnancy, the breast undergoes significant changes characterized by further duct and lobule proliferation, along with epithelial growth, predominantly through an increase in the number of alveoli per lobule.

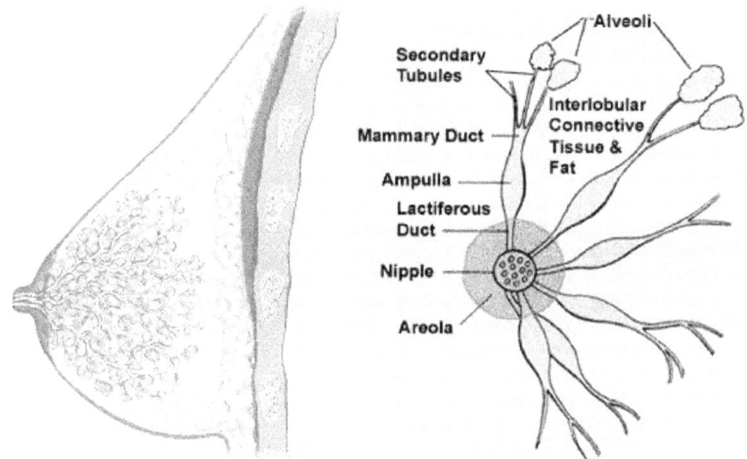

Longitudinal Section and Functional anatomy of Lactating Breast

By the sixth month of pregnancy, these changes are completed, and the breast expands further due to increased blood flow and secretion of colostrum. Each breast gains approximately 400 grams in weight during pregnancy.

True lactation begins within 1–4 days after childbirth and can continue for up to 3 years with regular breastfeeding. Upon weaning, there is progressive atrophy of the lobules and ducts, often replaced by fatty tissue.

Changes also occur during the menstrual cycle, with breast size increasing around mid-cycle due to heightened blood flow, leading to greater hydration of stromal tissue. Minor structural changes in epithelial tissue occur during the luteal phase of the cycle (second half).

With age, the proportions of breast components change, and after menopause, there is glandular tissue involution, sometimes replaced by adipose tissue, resulting in decreased breast volume. Additionally, various mechanical properties such as elasticity of connective tissue supporting the breast undergo alterations over time.

Functions of the Breast

1. Breastfeeding

The primary function of mammary glands is to nourish infants by producing breast milk, a process known as lactation. Breastfeeding provides essential nutrients and immune factors crucial for infant growth and development.

2. Sexual Role

Breasts play a significant role in human sexual behavior and are prominent female secondary sex characteristics. They are sensitive to touch due to numerous nerve endings. Oral stimulation of nipples and breasts is also a common aspect of sexual activity, contributing to sexual pleasure and intimacy.

Hormonal Control of Breast Development and Lactation

During puberty, there is no histological or functional difference in the breasts of pre-pubertal boys and girls. However, profound sexual dimorphism in breast development occurs at this time.

Growth of the Female Breast at Puberty

The growth of female breasts is primarily mediated by estradiol, which stimulates the enlargement, division, and elongation of the tubular duct system and the maturation of nipples. Interestingly, administration of estrogen to men is equally effective in inducing breast growth.

For true alveolar development at the ends of the ducts, the synergistic action of progesterone is required. Within the gland, various mediators influence epithelial cell division and differentiation. These mediators include:

Stimulatory Factors

- Insulin-like growth factors
- Transforming growth factor
- Epidermal growth factor

Inhibitory Factors

- Transforming growth factor

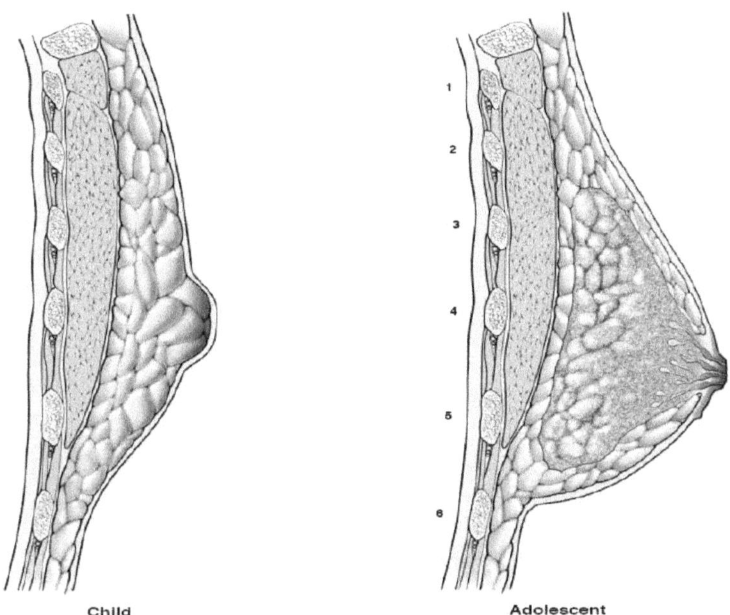

Mammary glands of prepubertal girl and the adolescent

(a- In prepubertal girl, the mammary glands grow and branch slowly, b- In adolescence the mammary glands develop rapidly, with the growth of the duct system influenced by estrogen and progesterone)

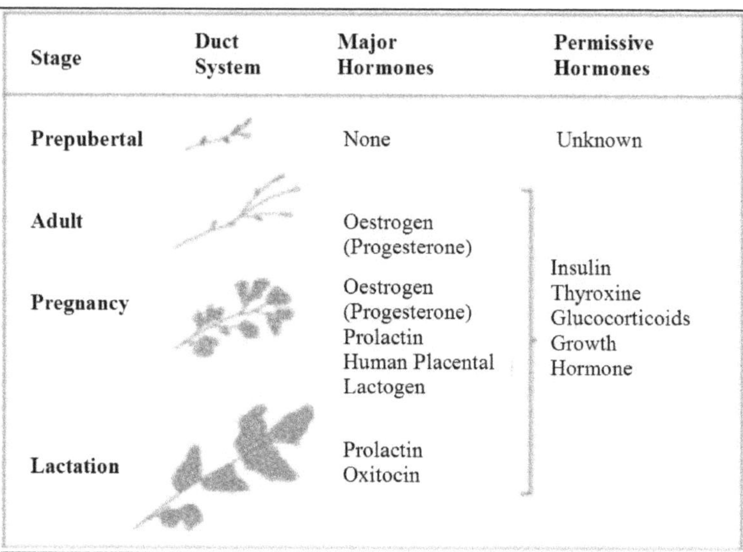

Stage	Duct System	Major Hormones	Permissive Hormones
Prepubertal		None	Unknown
Adult		Oestrogen (Progesterone)	Insulin Thyroxine Glucocorticoids Growth Hormone
Pregnancy		Oestrogen (Progesterone) Prolactin Human Placental Lactogen	
Lactation		Prolactin Oxitocin	

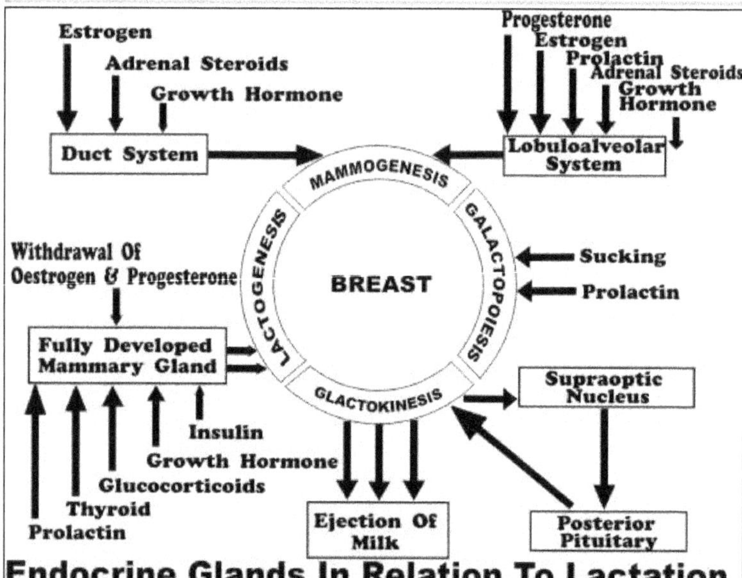

The endocrine control of Breast

 Dr. Rajneesh Kumar Sharma

Once the anatomic development of the ducts and alveoli is complete, the continued action of estrogen and progesterone is not required for lactation itself. However, normal breast development requires a complex interplay of hormones and growth factors.

Cyclic Changes during the Menstrual Cycle

During the normal menstrual cycle, cyclic changes in estrogen and progesterone levels result in the continued development of breast structures. As estrogen and progesterone levels decline near the end of the cycle, prolactin-induced secretory changes become evident in the alveolar lumen during the first few days of menstruation. The breasts are largest in this phase and smallest on days 4 to 7 of the cycle, making it the ideal time for breast self-examination.

Breast Changes during Pregnancy

Differentiation of the breast to its mature functional status occurs by the third month of pregnancy. The true glandular acini (alveoli) develop under the influence of several hormones, including prolactin, human placental lactogen, estradiol, progesterone, insulin, cortisol, growth hormone, IGF-1, and EGF. Thyroid hormones also promote alveolar growth.

Role of Prolactin in Lactation

In humans, prolactin acts to:

- Increase arginase activity

- Stimulate ornithine decarboxylase activity
- Enhance the rate of transport of polyamines into the mammary gland

These actions result in increased spermine and spermidine synthesis (polyamines), which are required for milk production. Prolactin also elicits increased messages and synthesis of casein, spermidine, lactose, and phospholipids, all of which are necessary for lactation.

Role of Progesterone

Progesterone interferes with prolactin action at the alveolar cell's prolactin receptor level. Although estrogen and progesterone are required for the full activity of the prolactin receptor, progesterone antagonizes the positive action of prolactin on its receptor by:

- Inhibiting upregulation of the prolactin receptor
- Reducing estrogen binding (lactogenic) activity
- Competing for binding at the glucocorticoid receptor

Initiation of Lactation

Actual lactation occurs after birth by allowing prolonged elevation of prolactin without progesterone inhibition due to the more rapid clearance of progesterone compared to prolactin. It takes approximately seven days for prolactin to reach non-pregnant levels postpartum, while estrogen and

 Dr. Rajneesh Kumar Sharma

progesterone elevations are cleared in three to four days.

Prolactin Levels Postpartum

In the first week postpartum, prolactin levels decline by 50% to about 100 ng/ml. Suckling increases prolactin levels, which is crucial for initiating lactation. Basal prolactin levels remain normal or slightly elevated with a twofold increase during suckling in the third to sixth months postpartum. Increased prolactin levels are required for lactogenesis; however, non-pregnant levels are sufficient to maintain lactation.

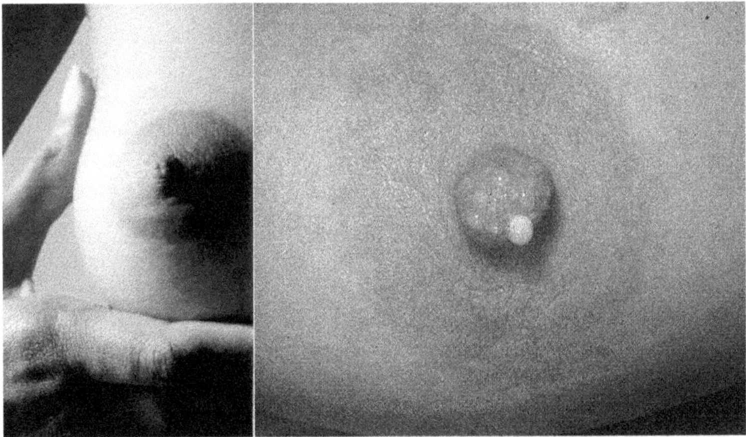

The Lactating Breasts Showing well developed Areola and Erected Nipple

Progesterone and Lactation

Postpartum, progesterone's effect diminishes as lactation begins due to a significant decrease in progesterone receptors. Progesterone, which has a higher affinity for milk fat than for the progesterone receptor, is rapidly cleared once lactation is initiated.

Inhibition of Lactation

Medically, lactation can be inhibited postpartum using bromocriptine, a dopamine agonist administered at 2.5 mg bid for two weeks. However, caution is necessary, especially in women with hypertension. Alternative methods like breast-binding, ice application, and avoiding nipple stimulation can also halt lactation within one week.

Breast Changes after Menopause

During menopause, when estrogen and progesterone production declines, breasts undergo changes in structure. Some women experience increased breast tenderness and lumpiness, possibly forming cysts.

Physiology of Lactation

Lactation, the formation of breast milk postpartum, begins after delivery but preparations for effective lactation occur during pregnancy.

Types of Milk Production Disorders

- **Hypolactation or Galactostasis**: Deficiency in milk production.
- **Agalactia**: Complete absence of lactation.
- **Galactacrasia**: Abnormal composition of mother's milk.

Stages of Lactation Understanding the physiology of lactation involves four stages:

1. **Mammogenesis**: Preparation of breasts for lactation.
2. **Lactogenesis**: Synthesis and secretion of milk from breast alveoli.
3. **Galactokinesis**: Ejection of milk outside the breast.
4. **Galactopoiesis**: Maintenance of lactation.

Each stage is crucial for successful breastfeeding, involving hormonal regulation, milk synthesis, and milk ejection. The complex interplay of hormones and physiological processes ensures adequate milk production and sustenance of lactation for infant nourishment.

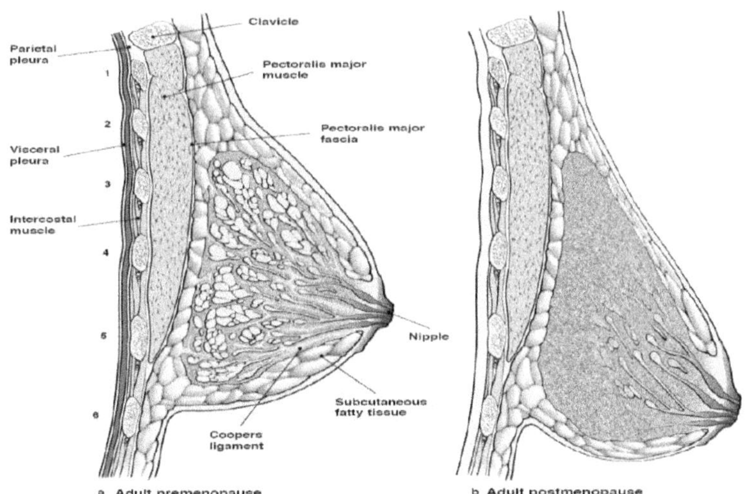

A- The adult premenopausal breast.
B- The adult postmenopausal breast

Synthesis and Secretion of Milk

Milk is synthesized and stored within alveolar units of the breast. The process of milk removal from the alveoli is facilitated by the contraction of myoepithelial cells surrounding the alveoli and ducts, a mechanism known as milk ejection.

Milk Pathway

After production, milk exits through ductules into ducts that drain multiple clusters of alveoli. These small ducts merge to form 15 to 25 main ducts, each draining specific sectors of the gland. As these main ducts approach the areola, they widen into small sinuses, ultimately opening directly onto the nipple.

Breast Tissue Composition

The mammary ducts and alveoli are embedded within a stroma composed of various cellular components:

- **Fibroblasts**: Provide structural support to the breast tissue.
- **Adipocytes**: Store fat and contribute to breast volume and shape.
- **Plasma Cells**: Produce antibodies essential for immune defense.
- **Blood Vessels**: Ensure nutrient delivery and waste removal essential for milk production.

This stromal environment supports the functional integrity of the breast and provides the necessary framework for milk synthesis, storage, and release.

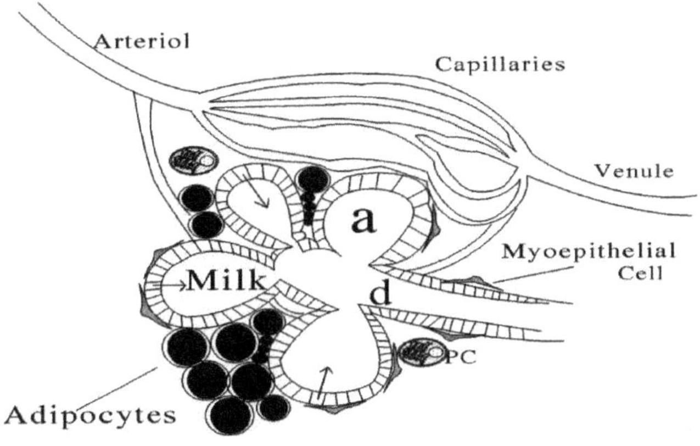

Model alveolus with subtending duct (d) showing blood supply, adipocyte stroma, myoepithelial cells, and plasma cells (PC)

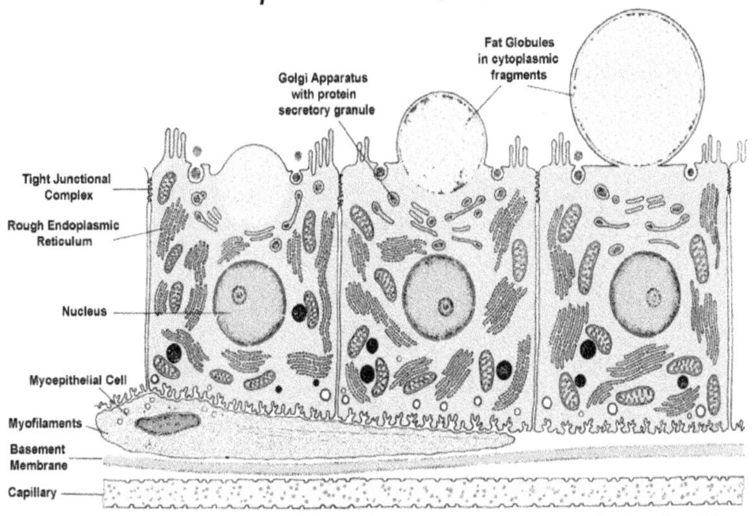

Milk production by alveolar secretory epithelial cells

Synthesis and Secretion of Breast Milk

During lactation, extensive blood flow is directed to the breast to provide the necessary substrates for milk synthesis. The interactions with stromal cells play a crucial role in mammary development and milk secretion. Stromal fibroblasts or adipocytes act as sources of growth factors like hepatic growth factor/scatter factor and IGF-1, and they likely produce lipoprotein lipase, essential for milk lipid synthesis. Additionally, B lymphocytes migrate to the mammary gland during lactation, where they transform into plasma cells and produce immunoglobulins that are incorporated into the milk.

Processes Involved in Milk Secretion

1. **Exocytosis**
   - The majority of milk components are secreted via exocytosis. Proteins synthesized on ribosomes are transferred to the lumen of the rough endoplasmic reticulum, where signal sequences are cleaved and proteins are folded.
   - Vesicles transport proteins to the Golgi stack for further processing, including addition of carbohydrate, phosphate, or other groups. The processed proteins are packaged into secretory vesicles.
   - Lactose synthesis occurs in the Golgi vesicles from UDP-galactose and glucose, with water drawn into the vesicles due to

lactose impermeability, leading to vesicle swelling.

- o Casein micelle formation begins in the Golgi, followed by calcium-mediated maturation of micelles in secretory vesicles.
- o Secretory vesicles fuse with the plasma membrane and release their contents into the milk space via exocytosis.

2. **Lipid Synthesis and Secretion**
   - o Triglycerides are synthesized in the smooth endoplasmic reticulum, forming large droplets that coalesce and become enveloped by the apical plasma membrane.
   - o The lipid droplets, encased in membrane, are released as milk fat globules. The membrane serves as a source of dietary phospholipids and cholesterol for the infant, while preventing coalescence of fat droplets.

3. **Transport across Apical Membrane**
   - o Apical pathways facilitate transport of small molecules. Many drugs enter milk directly through both basolateral and apical membranes of mammary alveolar cells.

4. **Transcytosis of Interstitial Molecules**
   - o Intact proteins cross the mammary epithelium via transcytosis during lactation. Immunoglobulins are transported through a receptor-mediated process, forming IgA-receptor complexes

that are endocytosed and transferred across the cell to the apical membrane.
  - The extracellular portion of the receptor is cleaved at the apical membrane, releasing secretory IgA (sIgA) into milk.

5. **Paracellular Pathway**
  - The paracellular pathway allows passage of substances between epithelial cells via tight junctions (Zonula occludens).

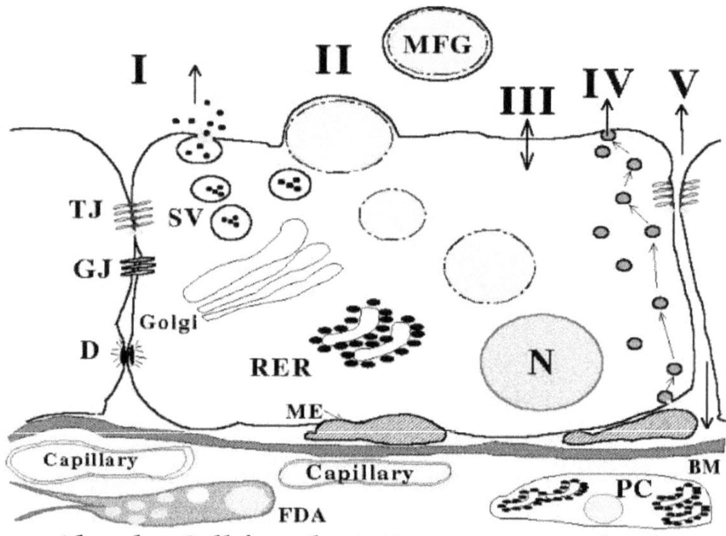

Alveolar Cell from lactating mammary gland
(N, nucleus; TJ, tight junction; GJ, gap junction; D, desmosome; SV, secretory vesicle; FDA, fat-depleted adipocyte; PC, Plasma Cell; BM, basement membrane; ME, cross section through process of myoepithelial cell; RER, rough endoplasmic reticulum. See text for explanation of secretory pathways I (exocytosis), II (lipid), III (apical transport), IV (transcytosis) and V (paracellular pathway)

- o Tight junctions impede movement between cells during lactation but become leaky during pregnancy, mastitis, and involution, allowing substances to pass between cells.
- o Leaky junctions during mastitis and involution facilitate removal of secretion products, entry of immune cells and protective molecules into milk, and clearance of mammary cell dissolution products.
- o High sodium and chloride concentrations in milk during open junction periods can aid in diagnosing breastfeeding issues.

LACTOGENESIS

It is the transition from pregnancy to lactation. Formally lactogenesis was defined as the onset of milk secretion. It is divided into two stages.

Lactogenesis Stage 1-
It occurs during pregnancy when the gland becomes sufficiently differentiated to secrete small quantities of specific milk components such as casein and lactose.

Lactogenesis Stage 2-

It is defined as the onset of copious milk secretion associated with parturition. It is brought about by a decline in progesterone around the time of parturition in the presence of maintained prolactin concentrations. A differentiated mammary epithelium is necessary for this stage of lactogenesis to occur. In humans the epithelium reaches this stage of differentiation about mid-pregnancy.

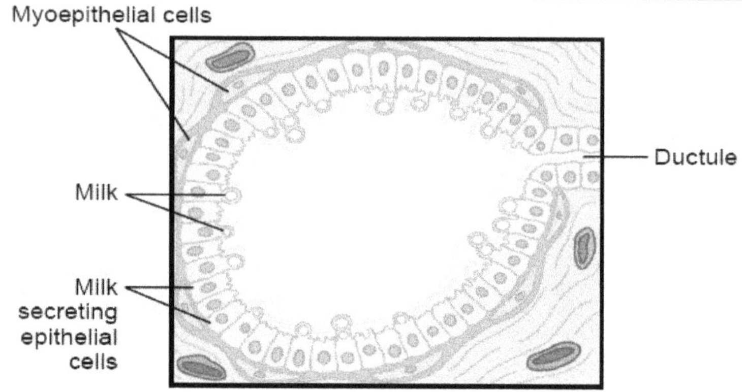

Milk-secreting cells of an alveolus

Colostrum-

In the early post-partum period the secretion product of the mammary gland is called colostrum. This fluid contains high concentrations of immunoglobulins and the protective protein, lactoferrin.

The presence of secretory IgA, lactoferrin and high concentrations of oligosaccharides is important in protection of mucosal surfaces from infection.

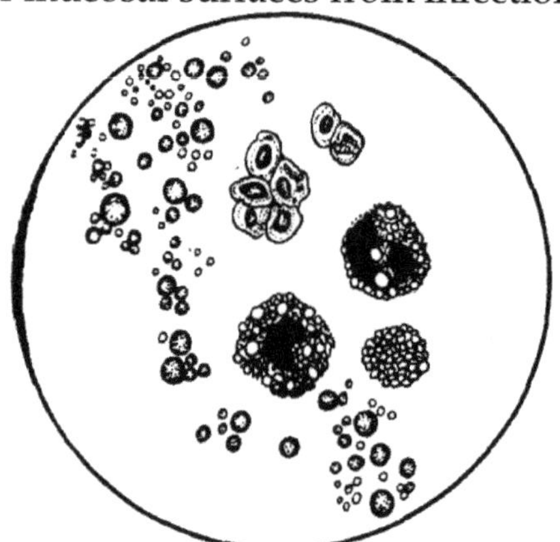

Microscopic picture of colostrum
(Fat droplets and colostrum corpuscles can be seen)

Colostrum may be defined as the foremilk, a thin white opalescent fluid, the first milk secreted at the termination of pregnancy differing from the milk secreted later by containing more lactalbumin and lactoprotein.

Colostral milk is markedly different, poor in nutrients with an ionic composition like blood plasma.

It reacts alkaline, and contains proteins, fats, epithelial cells of the glandular vesicles and the lactiferous ducts) and leucocytes containing fat droplets.

Finally, starting about 36 hours postpartum there is a 10-fold increase in milk volume from about 50 ml/day to 500 ml/day. This volume increase is perceived by the parturient woman as the "coming in" of the milk and is brought about by a massive increase in the rates of synthesis and/or secretion of almost all the components of mature milk.

The endocrine control of Lactation

It is complex process. It requires appropriate priming by estrogen and progesterone along with lactogenic hormones. To complete process of lactation, the permissive action of glucocorticoid, insulin, thyroxine, and, in some species, growth hormone is also necessary.

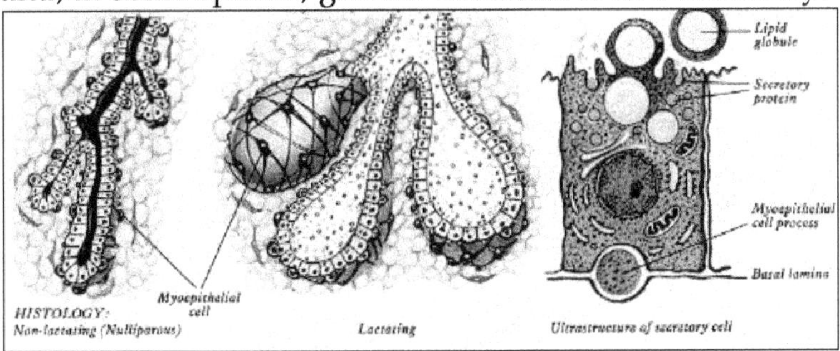

The Nonlactating and Lactating Alveoli

There are two lactogenic hormones:

Chorionic somatomammotropin or Human placental lactogen-

Human placental lactogen or hPL is secreted in large amounts by the placenta during the latter part of gestation and prepares the breast for milk production. It disappears from the maternal and fetal circulation shortly after termination of pregnancy.

Prolactin-

Prolactin is a tetrahelical cytokine most closely related to growth hormone and placental lactogens. It binds to specific prolactin receptors that belong to the WS-motif cytokine receptor family.

Prolactin is secreted in a highly regulated manner into the circulation by the anterior pituitary, and acts on peripheral target tissues as a hormone.

In addition, prolactin is expressed at many extrapituitary sites, particularly within the female and male reproductive organs and the cells of the immune system, acting locally as an autocrine or paracrine cytokine. Because of the ubiquitous expression of prolactin receptors, prolactin has a wide range of cellular and physiological effects. In mammals, prolactin is particularly critical for the differentiation of the mammary gland and for lactation.

Hyperprolactinemia, the most common pituitary disorder, causes infertility and decreased libido in both men and women. Prolactin may also influence the progression of certain autoimmune diseases, and has been implicated as a promoter of neoplastic growth.

Chemistry of prolactin

Human PRL is a globular protein of a 199 amino acid single chain polypeptide and three intrachain disulfide bridges, encoded by a gene on chromosome 6. It has a molecular weight of 23000.

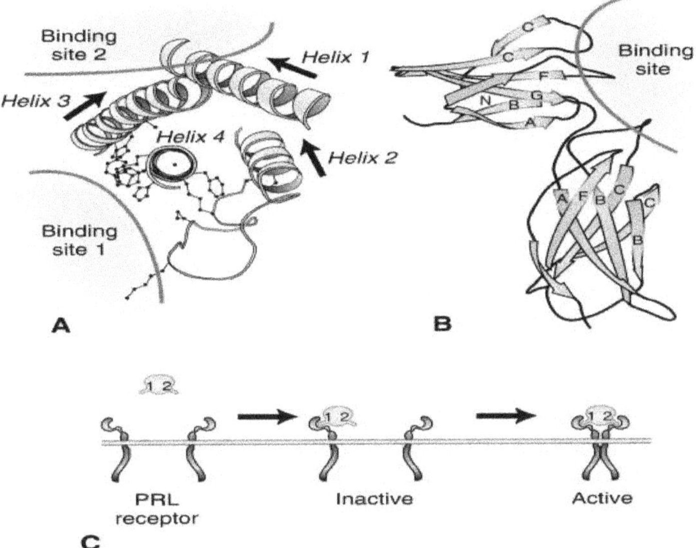

Molecular structure of prolactin (PRL) and its interaction with the receptor dimeric

It is synthesised in ribosomes and rough endoplasmic reticulum of lactotrophs of the adenohypophysis. It is concentrated in the Golgi apparatus and stored in cytoplasmic granules.

Secretion occurs in a sleep-related circadian rhythm in both males and females. Hypothalamic control of secretion is primarily inhibitory, mediated by PRL-release-inhibiting factor (dopamine). Thyrotrophin releasing hormone stimulates PRL secretion. The plasma half-life is 15–20 minutes. The actions are mediated by a dimeric tyrosine kinase-linked receptor.

Secretion of Prolactin

Prolactin secretion is crucial during pregnancy and lactation, orchestrated by various physiological stimuli and controlled by the hypothalamus. Here's an improved breakdown of the processes involved:

Prolactin Secretion Overview

- **Role in Lactation**: Prolactin secretion rises significantly during late pregnancy and plays a key role in initiating and sustaining lactation postpartum.
- **Pituitary Composition**: During late pregnancy and lactation, a significant portion (60-80%) of the anterior pituitary consists of Prolactin-secreting lactotrope cells due to the stimulating effects of estrogen.

Evaluation and Control of Prolactin Levels

- **Physiological Alterations**: Prolactin levels can be transiently or persistently elevated due to various physiological conditions and drug-related factors, often not requiring intervention.
- **Prolactin Levels**:
  - Normal plasma levels range from 5-27 ng/ml during the menstrual cycle.
  - Levels exhibit a pulsatile pattern, with frequency ranging from approximately 14 pulses per 24 hours in the late follicular phase to about nine pulses per 24 hours in the late luteal phase.

- o Diurnal variation: Lowest levels occur mid-morning post-awakening, rising within an hour of sleep onset.

Control Mechanisms of Prolactin Secretion

- **Hypothalamic Influence**: The hypothalamus regulates pituitary Prolactin secretion via:
    - o Dopamine-mediated tonic inhibition: Basal secretion is predominantly regulated by inhibitory hypothalamic hormones like dopamine.
    - o Suckling reflex: Stimulation of the breasts during nursing triggers a reflex release of oxytocin, indirectly enhancing Prolactin secretion.
- **Prolactin Receptors**: Prolactin binds to specific receptors on breast acinar cells, activating the JAK-STAT signal transduction pathway to stimulate milk synthesis.

Milk Production Postpartum

- **Milk Composition**: Postgestational lactating women produce approximately 1 liter of milk per day containing essential nutrients:
    - o Fat: 38 g
    - o Lactose: 70 g
    - o Protein: 12 g

Patterns of Prolactin Release

- **Circadian Rhythm**:

- o Prolactin levels peak during sleep and are lowest during waking hours, regulated by the suprachiasmatic nuclei of the hypothalamus.
- **Reproductive States**:
  - o **Lactation**: Suckling stimulus by nursing young is a primary physiological trigger for prolactin secretion.
  - o **Estrous and Menstrual Cycles**: Prolactin secretion remains low and stable during most of the estrous cycle, surging preovulation similar to LH.
  - o **Mating and Pregnancy**: Mating stimuli elevate and maintain prolactin secretion independent of ovarian steroids.

Prolactin Release in Response to External Stimuli

- **Light**: Circadian and seasonal variations influence prolactin secretion.
- **Audition and Olfaction**: Specific sounds and olfactory stimuli robustly affect prolactin secretion.
- **Stress**: Various stressors impact prolactin secretion, altering levels significantly.

Inhibition of Milk Ejection

- **Psychogenic Factors**: Generalized sympathetic nervous system stimulation can inhibit oxytocin secretion and depress milk ejection.
- **Suppression Methods**:

- o Estrogen administration or dopamine agonists like bromocriptine can suppress Prolactin secretion, inhibiting milk production.
- o Non-nursing postpartum leads to natural cessation of lactation within 1-2 weeks.

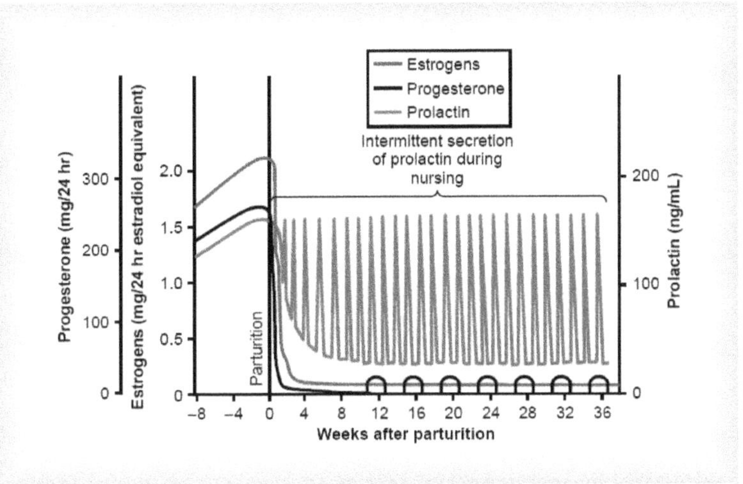

Changes in rates of secretion of estrogens, progesterone, and prolactin for 8 weeks before parturition and 36 weeks thereafter

(Noteworthy, especially, is the decrease of prolactin secretion back to basal levels within a few weeks after parturition, but also the intermittent periods of marked PRL secretion (for about 1 hour at a time) during and after periods of nursing)

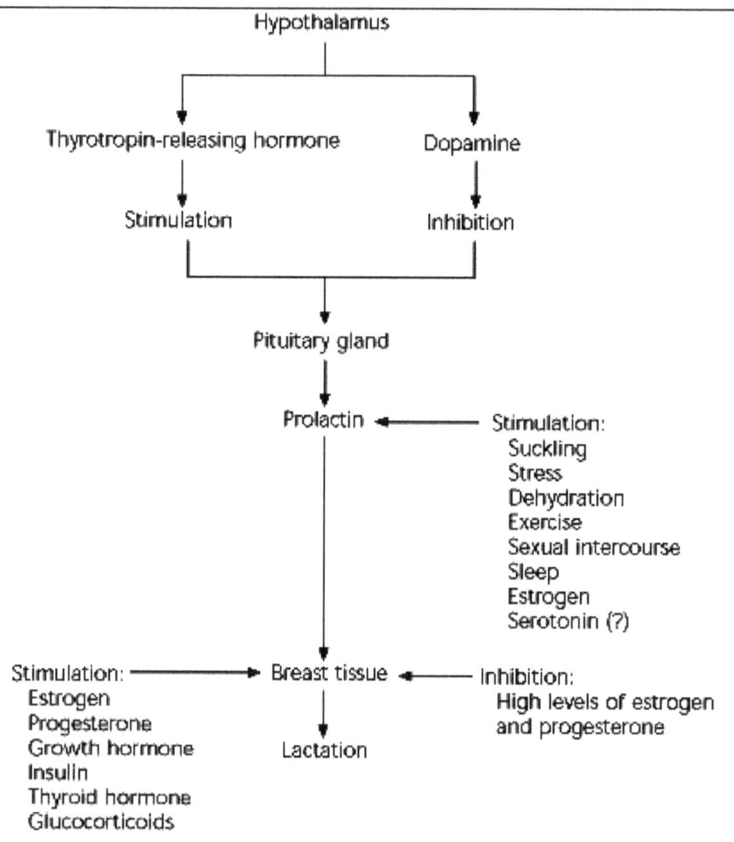

Physiology of lactation

Milk

Milk is a complex fluid. Breast milk is a white fluid (emulsion) in which minutest droplets of fat are suspended in serum. It is used in nourishment of the infant. The breast milk can be defined as a white liquid, containing proteins, sugar, and lipids, secreted by the mammary glands, and designed for the nourishment of the young.

Reaction- The milk reacts alkaline.

Specific gravity- 1.030

Boiling- It does not coagulate on boiling.

Composition of Human Milk

Human milk contains proteins 1.1 – 1.5 %, fat 2.5 - 4.8%, Lactose 6.0 - 7.1 %, ash 0.20 % and energy 293.0 Joule/ 100 ml.

Besides these, it also contains sodium 14.0 mg%, potassium 53.0 mg%, calcium 30.0 mg%, magnesium 4.0 mg%, iron 0.15 mg%, chlorides 30.0 mg%, phosphates 15.0 mg% and citric acid 120.0 mg% and a number of hormones as well as pharmacological substances taken in by mother.

Protein		Total	10.6 g/l
	Casein		
	Lactalbumin		
	Albumin		
	Immunoglobulin		
Carbohydrate		Total	78 g/l
	Lactose		71 g/l
	Oligosaccharides		6 g/l
	Fructose		1 g/l
Fats		Total	45.4 g/l
Water			897 g/l
Minerals			
	Sodium		172 mg/l
	Potassium		S12 mg/I
	Calcium		344 mg/l
	Magnesium		35 mg/l

Composition of Human milk

<u>Some Hormones and Their Concentrations in Human Milk</u>

Here are some hormones and their typical concentrations found in human milk:

Pituitary Hormones

- **Prolactin**: 20-90 ng/mL
- **Growth Hormone**: 5-30 uU/mL
- **Thyroid Stimulating Hormone (TSH)**: 2.7-5.0 uU/mL

Hypothalamic Hormones

- **Thyrotropin Releasing Hormone (TRH)**: 0.025-1.5 ng/mL
- **Luteinizing Hormone-Releasing Hormone (LHRH)**: Not Available
- **Somatostatin**: 23-113 pg/mL
- **Growth Hormone Releasing Hormone (GHRH)**: 23-430 pg/mL

Thyroid Hormones

- **Thyroxine (T4)**: 0.3-12 ng/mL
- **Triiodothyronine (T3)**: 0.2-0.4 ng/mL
- **Reverse T3**: 0.008-0.15 ng/mL

Parathyroid Hormones

- **Parathyroid Hormone (PTH)**: 15 pg/mL

- **Parathyroid Hormone Related Peptide:** 30-50 ng/mL
- **Calcitonin/Calcitonin Inhibiting Protein:** 0-5 ng/mL

Steroid Hormones

- **Estrogen:** 15-840 ng/mL
- **Progesterone:** 10-40 ng/mL
- **Adrenal Steroids:** 0.2-32 ng/mL

These concentrations provide a snapshot of the hormonal milieu present in human milk, influencing various aspects of infant development and metabolism.

Breast Milk

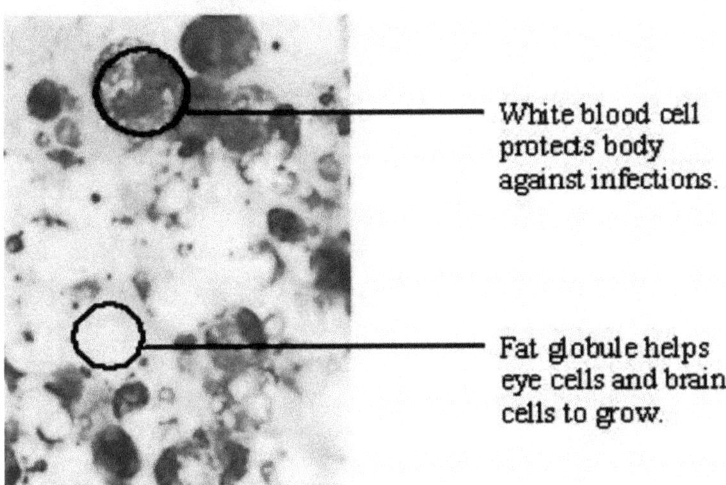

Microscopic picture of milk (Fat drops alone are seen)

<u>Galactorrhoea- An Overview</u>

Definition of 'Galactorrhoea'-

Various authors have defined Galactorrhoea in different ways-

- [galacto- + G. rhoia, a flow] Continuation of lactation or flow of milk at intervals after cessation of nursing. Excessive flow of milk.
- 'Galactorrhoea' can be defined as inappropriate production of milk that is persistent or worrisome to the patient, recognizing that in some instances no underlying pathology may be demonstrated.
- Any white discharge from the nipple that is persistent and looks like milk.
- Continued discharge of milk from the breasts between intervals of nursing or after the child has been weaned.
- 'Galactorrhoea' refers to the nonpuerperal discharge of milk-containing fluid from the breast.
- 'Haziq', an Urdu Medical Book and 'Jeby Haqeem', an Urdu Medical Book By Haqeem Mohammad Abdul Rehman, 28-04-1938 ed. say that Galactorrhoea is excessive milk discharge from the nipple due to abnormal exercise of the breast system.

Synonyms and Related Terms for 'Galactorrhea'

Here are synonyms and related terms associated with 'galactorrhea':

1. Incontinence of Milk
2. Amenorrhea-Galactorrhea-FSH Decrease Syndrome

3. Argonz-Del Castillo Syndrome
4. Galactorrhea-Amenorrhea without Pregnancy
5. Nonpuerperal Galactorrhea-Amenorrhea
6. Ahumada-del Castillo Syndrome
7. Argonz-Ahumada-Del Castillo Syndrome
8. Chiari's Syndrome II
9. Chiari-Frommel Syndrome
10. Forbes-Albright Syndrome
11. Frommel's Disease

These terms describe various clinical conditions associated with galactorrhea and amenorrhea, reflecting different etiologies and presentations of this hormonal disorder.

Epidemiology of 'Galactorrhoea'-

According to Harrison's Principles of Internal Medicine, 11th Edition, in one fourth patients with 'Galactorrhoea', a pituitary tumor was identified. Other known causes were identified in another fourth or fifth, and the remaining half felt into the idiopathic category. Many of the later group ultimately developed Prolactin-secreting pituitary tumors, some probably had subtle disorders of hypothalamic function, and in others a drug-related cause may have been missed.

The fact remains that no satisfactory diagnosis is reached in many patients. When menses are normal, the likelihood of establishing a cause for 'Galactorrhoea' is poor. 'Galactorrhoea' is unusual in men, even in the presence of profound elevations of plasma Prolactin; when it does occur, it is usually upon the background of a feminizing state.

 Dr. Rajneesh Kumar Sharma

In a study to ascertain "Role of Homoeopathy in Galactorrhoea with Miasmatic Analysis" with the intention of learning the facts about this disease and understanding the various concepts of Galactorrhoea especially in terms of Homoeopathy the effectiveness of Homoeopathic medicines in its treatment was analyzed and a comparative study of the results on the basis of various filters and protocols was made.

The follwing conclusions were derived from study.

Sex incidence-

Females are most affected than males. Males- 06%, Females 94%.

Age incidence-

The incidence of Galactorrhoea is maximum in age group of 31-40 years and least in prepuberty group.

Marital status incidence-

It was more in married patients (71%) than singles (29%).

Physical built incidence-

Maximum cases were recorded from thin built persons and least in moderate.

Occupational incidence-

The Galactorrhoea was prevalent mosty in House wives (50%), working patients (26%), Students (12%) and in non working (12%).

Socioeconomic incidence-

Galactorrhoea was most prevalant in rich persons (50%) and least in poors (09%).

Pathological incidence-

The most frequent was Idiopathic Galactorrhoea (35 %), The second one being Galactorrhoea with hypothyroidism (26 %), then Galactorrhoea amenorrhoea syndrome (15 %), then Galactorrhoea with pituitary tumours (15 %) and the least being Galactorrhoea with fibroadenoma (09 %).

Menstrual incidence-

It was maximum seen in the females without menses especially those with amenorrhoea rather than postmenopausal ones. In females with menses, it was mainly in normally menstruating ladies than those with scanty menses.

Miasmatic incidence-

The Psora was found to be the top ranking miasm causing Galactorrhoea (56%), the next being Psora associated with Sycosis (23%), Pseudopsora (18%), free Sycosis very rare (03%) and no cases were reported from Syphilis alone or Cancerous miasms.

Physiology of 'Galactorrhoea'-

Since the action of a lactogenic hormone is necessary for the initiation of milk production, it is logical to consider 'Galactorrhoea' as a consequence of deranged Prolactin physiology. However, a complex hormonal milieu is necessary for lactation. Milk production does not take place in many instances in which Prolactin is elevated, both in men and in women who have not been exposed to the necessary hormonal environment. As a consequence, hyperprolactinemia is more common than Galactorrhoea. Furthermore, while enhanced Prolactin secretion is necessary for the initiation of lactation, continued production can be maintained in the presence of minimally or intermittently elevated Prolactin levels so that basal plasma Prolactin levels are not always elevated in patients with Galactorrhoea. In some such women Prolactin levels may be elevated during sleep or with stimulation of the nipple; in others, hyperprolactinemia may have been present transiently. Perhaps the strongest evidence for a critical role for Prolactin in Galactorrhoea is the fact that administration of dopaminergic agents that suppress plasma Prolactin levels corrects Galactorrhoea even when the basal plasma Prolactin levels are normal.

Etiology of 'Galactorrhoea'

The main cause of Galactorrhoea is hyperprolactinemia. Hyperprolactnemia can be caused by numerous diversant lesions and insults. These include CNS injury at birth, encephalitis, meningitis, CNS trauma, granulomatous forming lesions such as syphilis and tuberculosis, acute arteritis, cavernous sinus thrombosis, infiltrative disorders such as histiocytosis X, various forms of head trauma, central dopamine dysfunction, lactotrophe hyperplasia, prolactinomas, endocrinopathies such as primary hypothyroidism, chest trauma and thoracotomy, breast augmentation or reduction, breast biopsy, herpes zoster, metabolic disorders such as renal failure, hysterectomy or oopherectomy and the injections of myriad of pharmaceutical products including birth control pills, tranquillizers, antidepressants, antihypertensives, isoniazid and cimetidine. The causes of Galactorrhoea can be categorized as under-

a. **Physiologic hypersecretion**

Galactorrhoea may be due to physiological hypersecretion of Prolactin during-

  i. Pregnancy

  ii. Lactation

  iii. Chest wall stimulation, herpes zoster, trauma or surgery

  iv. Sleep

  v. Stress

b. **Hypothalamic-pituitary stalk damage**

  i. **Tumors**

    1. **Craniopharyngioma-** a suprasellar neoplasm, which may be cystic, that develops from the nests of epithelium derived from Rathke pouch.

    2. **Suprasellar pituitary mass extension-** it may arise from a prolactinoma or craniopharyngioma.

    3. **Meningioma-** a benign, encapsulated neoplasm of arachnoidal origin, occurring most frequently in adults.

    4. **Dysgerminoma-** A malignant neoplasm of the ovary (counterpart of seminoma of the testis), composed of undifferentiated gonadal germinal cells and occurring more frequently in patients less than 20 years of age.

    5. **Chordoma-** A rare neoplasm of skeletal tissue in adults, derived from persistent portions of the notochord.

    6. **Hemangiopericytoma-** An uncommon vascular, usually benign, neoplasm

composed of round and spindle cells that are derived from the pericytes and surround endothelium-lined vessels.

7. **Metastases**

ii. **Empty sella-** it is defined as a pituitary sella which, regardless of its size, is completely or partly filled with cerebrospinal fluid. An empty sella of normal size is a frequent incidental autopsy finding and may be regarded as a normal anatomic variant. An empty sella is called "secondary" when it is seen after surgery, irradiation, or medical treatment of a pituitary pathology. Most patients have no pituitary dysfunction, but an empty sella may be associated with partial or complete pituitary insufficiency, pituitary hypersecretion, headache, and visual disturbances. The discovery of an empty sella needs to be followed by an endocrine evaluation to determine whether there is any associated pituitary dysfunction.

iii. **Lymphocytic hypophysitis-** an acute anterior pituitary lymphocytic reaction characterized clinically by signs and symptoms of anterior pituitary insufficiency.

iv. Adenoma with stalk compression

v. **Giant cell Granuloma-** a nonneoplastic lesion characterized by a proliferation of granulation tissue containing numerous multinucleated giant cells.

vi. **Sarcoidosis-** a systemic granulomatous disease of unknown cause, especially involving the lungs with resulting interstitial fibrosis, also affecting all the systems of the body including nervous system.

vii. Tuberculosis

Rathke's cyst- Rathke's pouch arises from an outpocketing of stomodeum (ectoderm) and gives rise to the adenohypohysis. Pharyngohypophyseal stalk, which connects the stomadeum and Rathke's pouch, is divided by the sphenoid bone as it grows together, isolating Rathke's pouch and the neurohypophysis within the sella. The anterior and intermediate lobes of the pituitary gland arise embryologically from Rathke's pouch. Inadequate pouch obliteration results in cysts or cystic remnants at the interface between the anterior and posterior pituitary lobes, which are found in about 20% of pituitary glands at autopsy. Pituitary adenomas also occasionally contain small cleft cysts. They are lined by cuboidal or columnar ciliated epithelium surrounding mucoid cyst fluid. They arise from midline rudiments of failed Rathke's cyst invagination and account for about 3% of pituitary mass lesions. In contrast, pituitary epidermoid cysts are lined by squamous epithelium, which rarely becomes malignant. Rathke's cysts vary in size and can also extend to the suprasellar region. Cyst formation is associated with sellar enlargement. These lesions rarely manifest with panhypopituitarism with or without diabetes insipidus. Most, however, are not symptomatic and should be followed expectantly. The extent of headache or visual disturbance is determined by the size and location of the cyst.

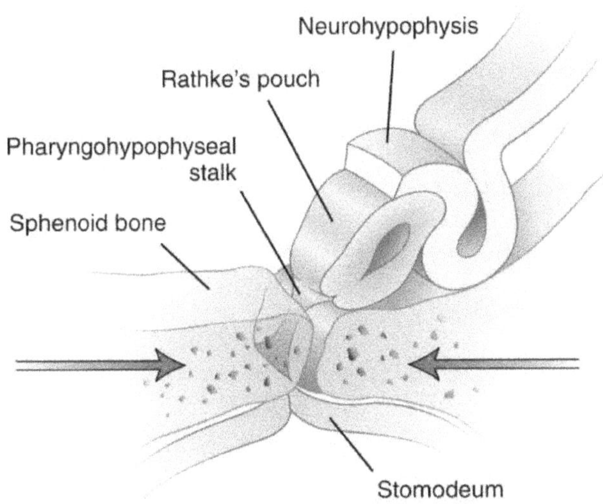

Pathogenesis of Rathke's cysts

(Schematic of the embryologic progenitors of sellar and parasellar structures)

   viii. Irradiation
    ix. Trauma
       1. Pituitary stalk section
       2. Suprasellar surgery

c. Pituitary hypersecretion
    i. Prolactinoma
   ii. Acromegaly

d. Systemic disorders
    i. Chronic renal failure
   ii. Hypothyroidism
  iii. Liver Cirrhosis
   iv. Pseudocyesis

    v. Epileptic seizures

e. Drug-induced hypersecretion

    i. Dopamine receptor blockers
1. Phenothiazines: chlorpromazine, perphenazine
2. Butyrophenones: haloperidol
3. Thioxanthenes
4. Metoclopramide

    ii. Dopamine synthesis inhibitors
1. $\square$-methyldopa

    iii. Catecholamine depletors
1. Reserpine

    iv. Opiates

    v. H2 antagonists
1. Cimetidine, ranitidine

    vi. Imipramines
1. Amitriptyline, amoxapine

    vii. Serotonin-reuptake inhibitors
1. Fluoxetine

    viii. Calcium channel blockers
1. Verapamil

    ix. Hormones
1. Estrogens
2. Antiandrogens

Signs and Symptoms Associated with 'Galactorrhoea'

In Women-

Generals- some patients may have symptoms of estrogen deficiency such as hot flushes.

Sexual Sphere- These include menstrual irregularities, mainly sparse, irregular or absent menstruation and decreased libido.

Sometimes infertility despite regular menses is seen. In many cases there are no symptoms other than the ''Galactorrhoea'', though women with excessive Prolactin often stop ovulating and menstruating.

Skin- increased body hair, or hirsuitism and acne.

Particulars- If a prolactinoma exists; it may also cause headache and visual disturbances.

Others- Signs and symptoms of any other underlying diseases such as brain tumor, Chronic Renal Failure, Hypothyroidism, liver cirrhosis etc. may also intervene 'Galactorrhoea'.

In Men-

Men may present with reduction in libido, impotence, infertility, loss of sexual hair and gynaecomastia.

Headache and visual disturbances may be seen in cases with Prolactinoma.

Galactorrhoea is associated with the Symptoms of Hyperprolactinemia	
Women	**Men**
Irregular menstruation	Impotence
Infertility	Infertility
Loss of libido	Loss of libido
Headache	Headache
Peripheral vision problems	Peripheral vision problems
Mood changes / depression	Mood changes/depression
Galactorrhoea	Galactorrhoea
Menopausal symptoms, even when estrogen is sufficient	Gynaecomastia
Corpus luteum dysfunction	
Signs of increased androgen levels	

 Dr. Rajneesh Kumar Sharma

<u>Classification of 'Galactorrhoea'</u>

The classification of Galactorrhoea is done on basis of the etiology.

1. **Failure of normal hypothalamic inhibition of prolactin release**

   a. **Pituitary stalk section-** Hypothalamic lesions such as craniopharyngioma, primary hypothalamic tumor, metastatic tumor, histiocytosis X, tuberculosis, sarcoidosis and empty sella syndrome, and pituitary stalk lesions-traumatic or secondary to the mass effects of sellar tumors-are infrequent but significant causes of 'Galactorrhoea'.

      These lesions destroy dopamine-producing neurons in the hypothalamus and block the passage of dopamine from the hypothalamus to the pituitary gland.

      This results in lifting of the inhibitory effect of dopamine on lactotrophs.

      1. Empty Sella
      2. Rathke's cyst

   b. **Drugs-**

      1. **Dopamine-receptor blockage-** Dopamine is the primary neuroendocrine inhibitor of the secretion of prolactin from the anterior pituitary gland.
         Dopamine produced by neurons in the arcuate nucleus of the hypothalamus is secreted into the hypothalamo-hypophysial blood vessels of the median eminence,

which supply the pituitary gland.

The lactotrope cells that produce prolactin, in the absence of dopamine, secrete prolactin continuously; dopamine inhibits this secretion. Thus, in the context of regulating prolactin secretion, dopamine is occasionally called prolactin-inhibiting factor (PIF), prolactin-inhibiting hormone (PIH), or prolactostatin.

Prolactin also seems to inhibit dopamine release, such as after orgasm, and is chiefly responsible for the refractory period.

"Dopamine Receptor Antagonists" increase prolactin production by inhibiting the action of dopamine on dopamine D 2 receptors on pituitary lactotrophs.

i. **Butyrophenones-** a group of derivatives of 4-phenylbutylamine that have neuroleptic activity; e.g., haloperidol.

ii. **Metoclopramide-** A gastrointestinal pro-motility agent.

iii. **Phenothiazines-** A compound formerly used extensively for the treatment of intestinal nematodes; without central nervous system depressant activity itself, it serves as the parent compound for synthesis of a large number of antipsychotic compounds, including chlorpromazine, thioridazine, perphenazine, and fluphenazine.

iv. **Risperidone-** a benzixoxazole derivative, a noble antipsychotic agent that has an extremely strong binding affinity for serotonin -5 HT_2 receptors.

2. **Selective serotonin reuptake inhibitors**

   i. **Sulpiride-** An antidepressant.
   ii. **Thioxanthenes-** A class of tricyclic compounds resembling phenothiazine, current use emphasizes the antipsychotic and antiemetic properties of this class.

3. **Tricyclic antidepressants-** a chemical group of antidepressant drugs that share a 3-ringed nucleus; e.g., amitriptyline, imipramine, desipramine, and nortriptyline.

4. **Dopamine-depleting agents-**

   i. **Methyldopa-** an antihypertensive agent, also used as the ethyl ester hydrochloride, with the same action and uses.
   ii. **Reserpine-** an ester alkaloid isolated from the root of certain species of Rauwolfia; it decreases the 5-hydroxytryptamine and catecholamine concentrations in the central nervous system and in peripheral tissues; used in conjunction with other hypotensive agents in the management of essential hypertension and useful as a tranquilizer in psychotic states.

5. **Inhibition of dopamine release-**

   i. **Codeine-** an alkaloid of opium, used as

an analgesic and antitussive.

   ii. **Heroin-** an alkaloid, prepared from morphine by acetylation; rapidly metabolized to morphine in the body; formerly used for the relief of cough.

   iii. **Morphine-** it is the major phenanthrene alkaloid of opium and produces a combination of depression and excitation in the central nervous system and some peripheral tissues. It is used as an analgesic, sedative, and anxiolytic.

6. **Histamine- receptor blockage-**
   i. **Cimetidine-** a histamine analogue and antagonist used to treat peptic ulcer and hypersecretory conditions by blocking histamine H2 receptor sites, thus inhibiting gastric acid secretion.

7. **Stimulation of lactotrophs-**
   i. **Oral contraceptives-** these are either progestogen- estrogen combinations (e.g. levonorgestrel- ethinylestradiol, norgestrael- ethinylestradiol, lynesterol- ethinylestradiol, northindrone- ethinylestradiol or ethynodiol- mestranol) or norethisterone enantate (hormone derivatives). Progestin has marked side effects especially in injectible form, viz. breast enlargement or Galactorrhoea. Levonorgestrel may cause breast tenderness.
   ii. **Verapamil-** a calcium channel blocking agent used to treat cardiac arrhythmias and angina pectoris.

c. **Central nervous system disease, including extrapituitary tumors and null cell adenomas of the pituitary-** Neurogenic stimulation may repress the secretion of hypothalamic Prolactin inhibitory factor, which results in hyperprolactinemia and 'Galactorrhoea'. Neurogenic causes of Galactorrhoea include chest surgery, burns, and herpes zoster that affect the chest wall. Galactorrhoea may develop as a complication of spinal cord injury. Chronic emotional stress may be a neurogenic cause of Galactorrhoea.

2. **Enhanced Prolactin release**

   a. **Hypothyroidism-** Primary hypothyroidism is a rare cause of 'Galactorrhoea' in children and adults. In patients with primary hypothyroidism, there is increased production of thyrotropin-releasing hormone, which may stimulate Prolactin release. Hyperprolactinemia also may result from decreased hypothalamic dopamine secretion and decreased metabolic clearance of Prolactin. Occasionally, Galactorrhoea may result from thyrotoxicosis, possibly because of an increase in estrogen-binding globulin or alterations in estrogen metabolism that change the free estrogen level.

   b. **Sucking reflex and breast trauma-** 'Galactorrhoea' may be caused by prolonged, intensive breast stimulation, such as from suckling, self-manipulation, or stimulation during sexual activity. Galactorrhoea caused by breast stimulation is more common in parous women but has been reported in virgins, postmenopausal women, and men. Stimuli are thought to pass along the intercostal nerves to the posterior column of the spinal cord, to the mesencephalon, and finally to the hypothalamus, where the secretion of Prolactin inhibitory factor is reduced.

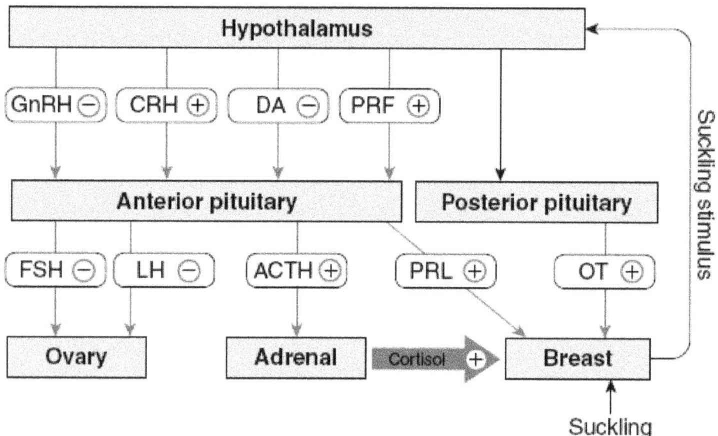

Effect of suckling on hypothalamic, pituitary, and adrenal hormones
(GnRH, gonadotropin-releasing hormone; CRH, corticotropin-releasing hormone; DA, dopamine; PRF, prolactin-releasing factor; FSH, follicle-stimulating hormone; LH, luteinizing hormone; ACTH, adrenocorticotropic hormone; PRL, prolactin; OT, oxytocin. '+' and '-' signs indicate positive and negative effects.)

Neurogenic stimulation may repress the secretion of hypothalamic Prolactin inhibitory factor, which results in hyperprolactinemia and Galactorrhoea. Neurogenic causes of

Galactorrhoea include chest surgery, burns, and herpes zoster that affect the chest wall. Galactorrhoea may develop as a complication of spinal cord injury. Chronic emotional stress may be a neurogenic cause of Galactorrhoea.

3. **Autonomous Prolactin release**

    a. **Pituitary tumors-** These are most common pathologic cause of 'Galactorrhoea'. These tumors can result in hyperprolactinemia by producing Prolactin or blocking the passage of dopamine from the hypothalamus to the pituitary gland.

    Prolactinomas are the most common type of pituitary tumor and are associated with Galactorrhoea, amenorrhea, and marked hyperprolactinemia. The serum level of Prolactin usually correlates with the size of the tumor. A minority of patients have gigantism/acromegaly with elevated levels of Prolactin and growth hormone.
    Macroprolactinomas are associated more often with visual field defects, headache, neurologic deficits, and loss of anterior pituitary hormones. These may be-

    1. **Prolactin-secreting tumors-** secreting micro- or macroadenomas.

    2. **Mixed growth hormone and Prolactin-secreting tumors-** These secrete both growth hormone and Prolactin and cause acromegaly with 'Galactorrhoea'.

3. **Null cell adenomas-** These may interfere with the delivery of dopamine to the pituitary, either by mass effects on the hypothalamus or by compressing the pituitary stalk.

b. **Ectopic production of human placental lactogen and/or prolactin**

1. **Hydatidiform moles and choriocarcinomas-** These may produce placental lactogen and may lead to 'Galactorrhoea'.

2. **Bronchogenic carcinoma and hypernephroma-** these may also contribute to 'Galactorrhoea' by secreting Prolactin Hormone.

4. **Insufficient clearing of Prolactin by Kidneys-** Approximately 30 percent of patients with chronic renal failure have elevated Prolactin levels, possibly because of decreased renal clearance of Prolactin.

5. **Hepatic cirrhosis-** Prolactin metabolism is hampered in cirrhotic liver leading to its progressive accumulation in blood. Liver cirrhosis also causes a 'Hepatorenal syndrome' which is a serious complication, characterized by ascitis, worsening azotemia with avid sodium retention and oliguria in the absence of identifiable specific causes of renal dysfunction. Worsening azotemia, hyponatremia, progressive oliguria, decreased peripheral PRL clearance and hypotension are the hallmarks of the Hepatorenal syndrome.

6. **Male 'Galactorrhoea'-** The phenomenon of male lactation in humans has become more common in recent years due to the use of medications that stimulate a man's mammary glands. Ordinarily there is so little mammary tissue that it is unnoticeable; if the male breasts develop visibly, the condition is called Gynaecomastia. Under the appropriate hormonal stimulus the mammary glands of human males can also produce milk. The volume of milk produced is low relative to that of a lactating female. Male lactation has, in some cases, commenced without hormonal treatments as well. Male lactation is most commonly caused by hormonal treatments given to men suffering from prostate cancer. Female hormones are used to slow the production of cancerous prostate tissue, but the same hormones also stimulate the mammary glands. Male-to-female transsexuals may also produce milk due to the hormones they take to reshape their bodies. Extreme stress combined with demanding physical activity and a shortage of food has also been known to cause male lactation.

7. **Infantile 'Galactorrhoea'-** Both male and female babies may lactate for a brief period immediately after birth because the baby gets a share of the hormones that were preparing the mother to lactate just prior to giving birth. For this reason, the baby's breasts also contain colostrum. High levels of estrogens in the placental-fetal circulation can result in Gynaecomastia in newborn infants. Enlargement of the breasts, which may be associated with secretion of milk (so-called "witch's

milk"), often is transient but may last longer in breastfed infants.

8. **Idiopathic-** Idiopathic 'Galactorrhoea' is a diagnosis of exclusion. Galactorrhoea is considered idiopathic if no cause is found after a thorough history, physical examination, and laboratory evaluation. The patient's breast tissue may have increased sensitivity to normal circulating Prolactin levels.

Types of breast discharges-

The discharge may be of following types-

- **Milky white-** It may be physiological, idiopathic, iatrogenic and pathological. The concentration of milk constituents may increase after repeated sampling.

- **Brown or greenish-** It rarely contains normal milk constituents and consequently may not result from an underlying endocrinopathy.

- **Bloody discharge-** It may be due to neoplasms of the breast.

Dr. Rajneesh Kumar Sharma

<u>Differential Diagnosis of 'Galactorrhoea'</u>

These include-

1- Failure of the normal hypothalamic inhibition of Prolactin release.

2- Increased Prolactin-releasing factor(s).

3- Autonomous Prolactin secretion by tumors.

4- Pituitary stalk section, traumatic or secondary to the mass effects of sellar tumors, results in increase in Prolactin secretion due to interruption in the delivery of dopamine to the pituitary.

5- Many drugs that influence the central nervous system (CNS) (including virtually all psychotropic agents, methyldopa, reserpine, and antiemetics) enhance prolactin release, presumably by inhibiting synthesis, release, or action of dopamine.

6- Estrogens increase prolactin secretion, but estrogen withdrawal (as in the discontinuation of oral contraceptives) may also trigger the onset of 'Galactorrhoea'.

7- CNS diseases outside the pituitary can cause 'Galactorrhoea' presumably by interfering with the production or delivery of dopamine to the pituitary (CNS sarcoidosis, craniopharyngioma, pinealoma, encephalitis, meningitis, hydrocephalus, hypothalamic tumors).

8- In primary hypothyroidism, 'Galactorrhoea' results from the enhanced production of thyrotropin-releasing hormone (TRH), which also stimulates prolactin release. Thyroid hormone replacement corrects the Galactorrhoea.

9- Chronic renal failure elevates PRL by decreasing peripheral PRL clearance.

10- Liver cirrhosis may cause Galactorrhoea by hampering further metabolism of prolactin in its damaged parenchyma.

11- A similar mechanism, involving enhanced secretion of oxytocin, may cause the 'Galactorrhoea' that follows breast surgery or breast trauma.

12- Enhanced prolactin release can also occur from pituitary or nonpituitary tumors. Three types of pituitary tumors can cause 'Galactorrhoea'-

    i.   Pure prolactin- secreting micro- or macroadenomas.

    ii. Mixed tumors- these secrete both growth hormone and prolactin and cause acromegaly with 'Galactorrhoea'.

    iii. Large null cell adenomas- These may interfere with the delivery of dopamine to the pituitary, either by mass effects on the hypothalamus or by compressing the pituitary stalk.

13- Occasionally, excess growth hormone secretion, in the absence of hyperprolactinemia causes 'Galactorrhoea'.

14- Rarely, prolactin is secreted by bronchogenic carcinomas.

15- Hydatidiform moles and choriocarcinomas may secrete placental lactogen.

16- **Ahumada- del Castillo syndrome-** A disorder characterized by 'Galactorrhoea' and amenorrhoea. Three types are reecognized:

    i.   **Chiari- Frommel syndrome:** persistent "Galactorrhoea" and amenorrhea after giving birth.

ii. **Ahumada- Del Castillo syndrome:**
Galactorrhoea-amenorrhoea not associated with
pregnancy, due to oestrogen deficiency and
decreased urinary gonadotropin levels.

iii. **Forbes- Albright syndrome:** Galactorrhoea-
amenorrhea caused by a chromophobe prolactin-
producing adenoma of the pituitary

Diagnostic Evaluation of Galactorhoea

Diagnostic tests may include-
- Medical history
- Physical examination
- Serum assays of Prolactin, FSH, LH, Estradiol, TSH etc.
- Chest X Ray
- CT or MRI of brain
- Mammography
- Visual field examination
- Renal failure or hepatic dysfunction should also be evaluated.

Physical Findings and Possible Etiology:

- **Poor growth:** Hypopituitarism, hypothyroidism, chronic renal failure
- **Gigantism/acromegaly:** Pituitary tumor
- **Bradycardia, goiter, coarse hair, dry skin, carotenoderma, myxedema:** Hypothyroidism
- **Tachycardia, goiter, hand tremor, exophthalmos:** Thyrotoxicosis
- **Visual field defect, papilledema, cranial neuropathy:** Pituitary tumor, intracranial mass
- **Hirsutism, acne:** Hyperandrogenism

These physical findings can provide important clues to the possible underlying causes when evaluating a patient with galactorrhea. Each presentation suggests specific etiologies that should be considered during physical examination and assessment.

Historical Evaluation of Patients with Galactorrhea-

When evaluating a patient with galactorrhea, it's important to consider the following symptoms and their potential underlying diagnoses:

- **Headache, visual disturbances, temperature intolerance, seizures, disordered appetite, polyuria, polydipsia**: These symptoms suggest possible pituitary or hypothalamic disease, such as a pituitary tumor affecting hormone production or regulation.
- **Decreased libido, infertility, oligomenorrhea or amenorrhea, impotence**: These symptoms are classic manifestations of hyperprolactinemia, where elevated levels of prolactin in the blood can disrupt normal reproductive hormone function.
- **Tiredness, cold intolerance, constipation**: These symptoms are typical of hypothyroidism, indicating an underactive thyroid gland that affects metabolism and other bodily functions.
- **Nervousness, restlessness, increased sweating, heat intolerance, weight loss despite increased appetite**: These symptoms are suggestive of thyrotoxicosis or hyperthyroidism, which occurs due to excessive thyroid hormone production.
- **Amenorrhea**: Absence of menstrual periods can be due to pregnancy or a pituitary tumor that disrupts the normal hormonal balance.
- **Medication use**: Some medications can induce galactorrhea as a side effect, so it's important to consider the patient's current medications.

- **Family history of thyroid disorder**: A family history of thyroid problems can indicate a genetic predisposition to thyroid dysfunction, which could be relevant to the patient's symptoms.
- **Family history of multiple endocrine neoplasia**: This suggests a potential genetic predisposition to tumors affecting multiple endocrine glands, including the pituitary gland.

A comprehensive evaluation involving a detailed medical history, thorough physical examination, and appropriate laboratory testing (including prolactin levels, thyroid function tests, and imaging studies if indicated) is essential to identify the underlying cause of galactorrhea and guide appropriate management and treatment. Consulting with an endocrinologist or a specialist in reproductive health can be beneficial in complex cases.

<u>Clinical Evaluation in Patients with Galactorrhea</u>

Patients presenting with galactorrhea should undergo careful and thorough evaluation, which includes the following aspects:

History:

- **Age of Onset:**
    - Onset in the neonatal period may indicate transplacental transfer of maternal estrogen leading to gynecomastia. Prolactinomas typically present in individuals aged 20 to 35 years.
- **Duration:**
    - Longer duration of galactorrhea without development of other clinical signs may suggest a lower likelihood of underlying organic disease.
- **Nipple Discharge:**
    - Galactorrhea typically presents as a milky discharge. Any bloody, serosanguineous, or purulent discharge should be considered pathological and distinguished from galactorrhea. Galactorrhea is usually bilateral, while pathological discharge is often unilateral. Note whether the discharge is scanty or abundant, expressed or spontaneous, and intermittent or persistent.
- **Gynecologic and Obstetric History:**
    - Obtain a detailed menstrual history and inquire about pregnancies, recent

abortions, and sexual activities. Amenorrhea could indicate pregnancy or a pituitary tumor. Hysterectomy or oophorectomy can elevate prolactin levels leading to galactorrhea.

- **Precipitating Factors:**
  - o Note any breast stimulation due to clothing, suckling, self-manipulation, or sexual activity. In infants, inquire about breastfeeding history, as galactorrhea is more common in breastfed infants.
- **Drug Use:**
  - o Gather a detailed drug history, as galactorrhea is associated with various medications that elevate serum prolactin levels. Common culprits include oral contraceptives, tranquillizers, antidepressants, antihypertensives, isoniazid, and cimetidine.

A comprehensive history helps identify potential causes of galactorrhea and guides further evaluation and management.

Personal History:

- Recent chest surgery and significant illnesses such as CNS injury at birth, encephalitis, meningitis, CNS trauma, granulomatous lesions (e.g., syphilis, tuberculosis), acute arteritis, cavernous sinus thrombosis, infiltrative disorders (e.g., histiocytosis X), various forms of head trauma, central dopamine dysfunction,

   Dr. Rajneesh Kumar Sharma

lactotroph hyperplasia, prolactinomas, and endocrinopathies (e.g., primary hypothyroidism).

History of chest trauma, thoracotomy, breast augmentation or reduction, breast biopsy, herpes zoster, metabolic disorders (e.g., renal failure), hysterectomy, or oophorectomy.

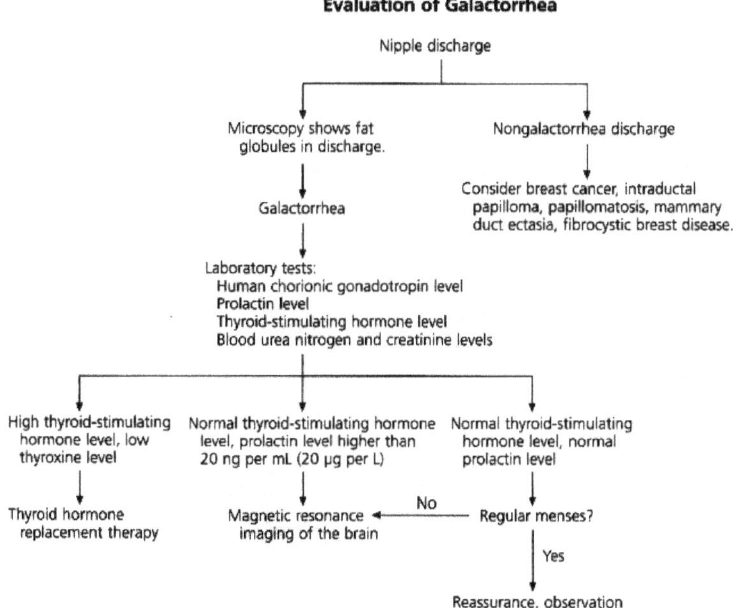

Family History:

- A family history of thyroid disorder or multiple endocrine neoplasia type I (MEN I) suggests a corresponding disorder. Approximately 30% of patients with MEN I have pituitary tumors, with prolactinoma being the most common.

Psychosocial History:

- Note any psychosocial stressors that may contribute to galactorrhea.

Physical Examination:

General:

- Assess weight, height, and vital signs. Poor growth may indicate hypopituitarism, hypothyroidism, or chronic renal failure.
- Gigantism/acromegaly suggests a pituitary tumor, while bradycardia suggests hypothyroidism and tachycardia suggests thyrotoxicosis.
- Inspect the chest for signs of local irritation, infection, previous surgery, or trauma.

Breast Examination:

- Conduct a thorough breast examination to identify nodules and assess for discharge. Determine whether the discharge is confined to one duct and note its location.
- Instruct patients on performing Breast Self-Exam (BSE) a few days after the menstrual period to ensure breasts are not tender. For non-menstruating individuals, perform BSE on the same day each month.

A detailed personal and family history, along with a comprehensive physical examination, helps identify potential causes of galactorrhea and guides further investigation and management.

Methods for Breast Self Exam or BSE-

1- Facing a mirror

While standing before a mirror comparison of both breasts for differences in size, nipple inversion (turning in), bulging, or dimpling is noted.
Any skin or nipple changes, such as a hard knot or nipple discharge are also noted.

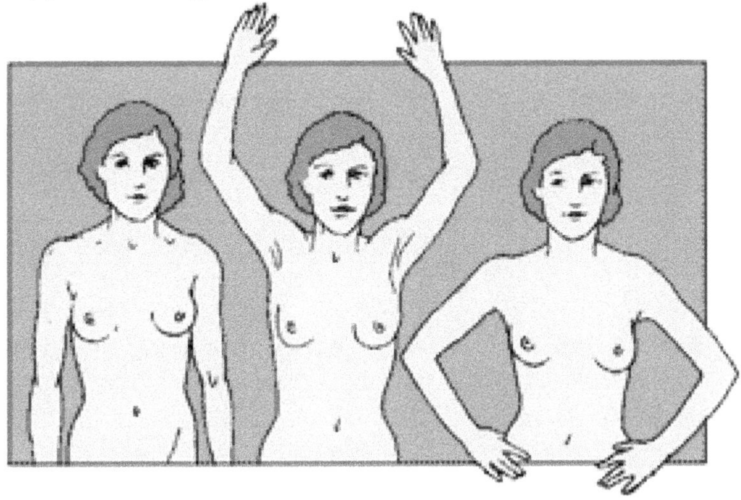

The breasts is inspected in the following 4 steps:
- With arms at sides
- With arms overhead
- With hands on hips - Pressing firmly to flex the chest muscles.
- Bending forward to inspect the breasts.

In these positions, the pectoral muscles are contracted, and a subtle dimpling of the skin may appear if a growing tumor has affected a ligament.

2- Lying down

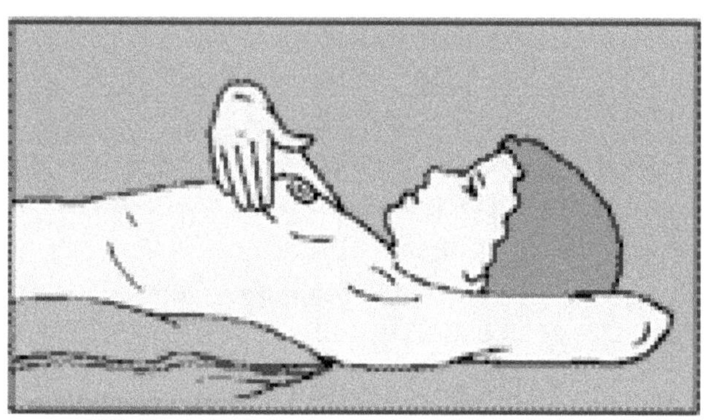

Right breast

- A pillow is placed under right shoulder.
- Right hand is put under the head.
- Entire breast area is checked with the finger pads of left hand.
- Small circles are used and an up-and-down pattern is followed.
- Light, medium, and firm pressure over each area of the breast is used.
- Breast is felt with the surfaces of the second, third, and fourth fingers, moving systematically and using small, circular motions from the nipple to the outer margins.
- Nipple is gently squeezed for any discharge.

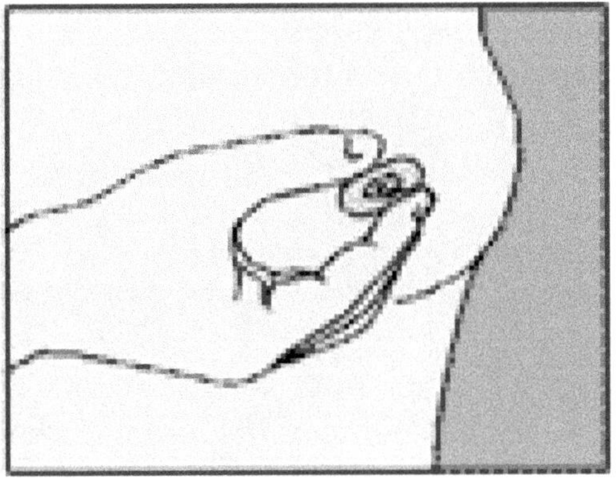

Left breast

- These steps are repeated on left breast using right hand.

3- In the shower

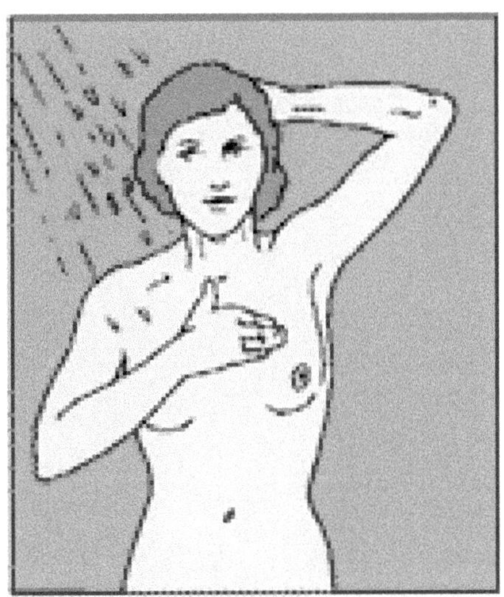

- A BSE can easily be performed while in the bath or shower. Some women discover breast masses when their skin is moist.

- Right arm is raised.
- With soapy hands and fingers flat, right breast is checked.
- Use of same small circles and up-and-down pattern is done as described earlier.
- On the left breast, the same is repeated.

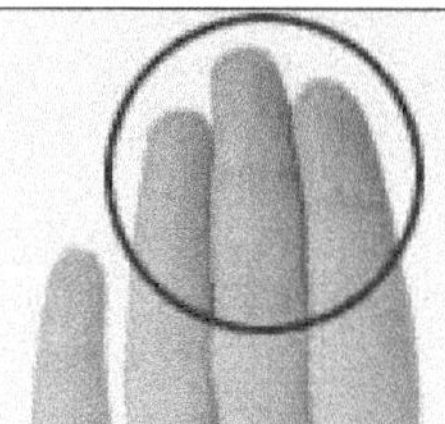

The pads of three middle fingers of the hand are used.

For the **clock pattern**, working is done way from the outer edge of the breast towards the nipple in small circles, going around the breast like the hands of a clock or spokes of a wheel.

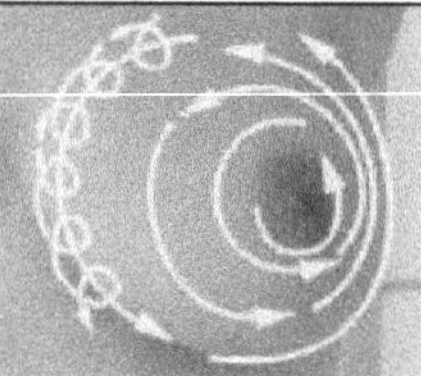

For the **circle pattern** feeling is done in a circle motion, starting at the outer area of the breast, working the way around the breast in smaller and smaller circles until getting the nipple. Feeling

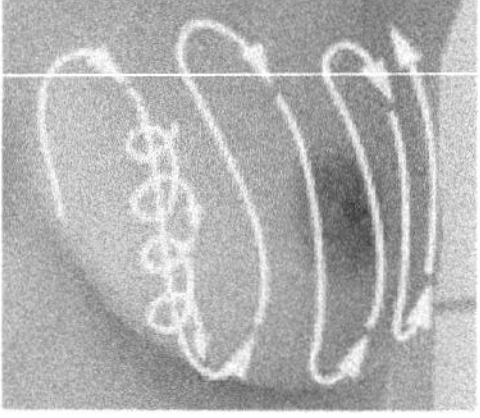

For the **grid pattern**, movement is done the fingers up and down the breast in rows, working the way from one side of the breast to the other.

is done in circles, like 1 ring inside another.	
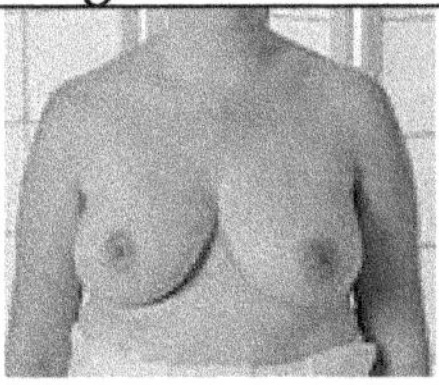 Standing or sittting upright	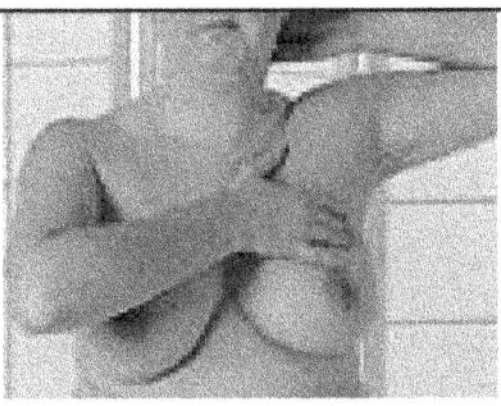 Putting one hand behind head
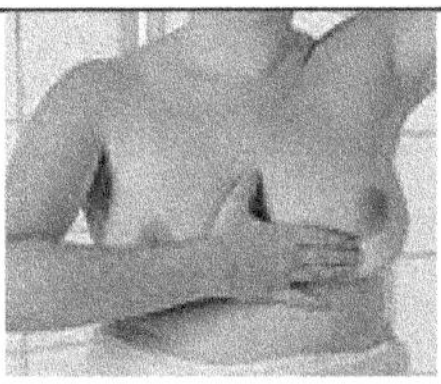 Entire breast area should be checked, using any pattern liking the best	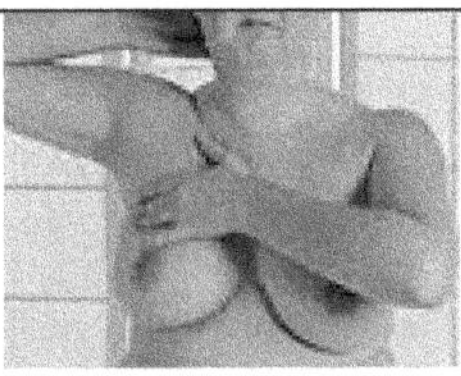 Switching arms and feeling other breast
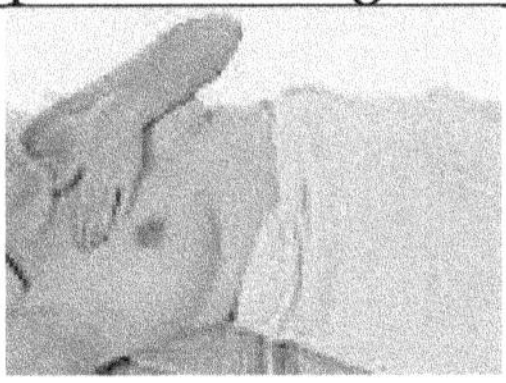 Lying down on back	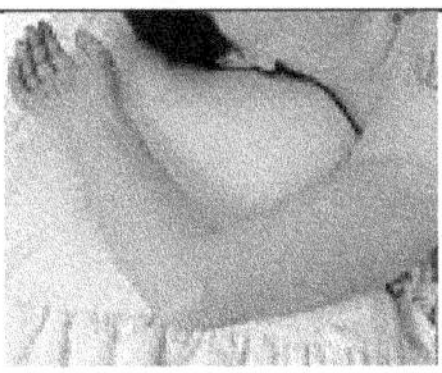 One hand behind head and other examining the breast.
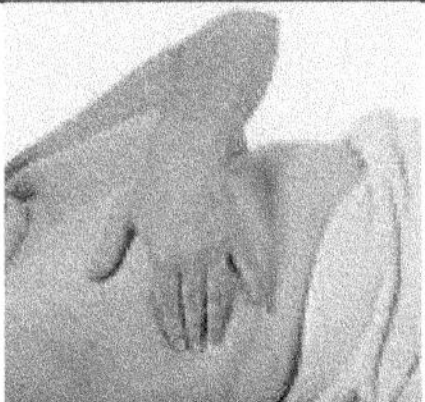 Checking the entire breast area. Switching arms and	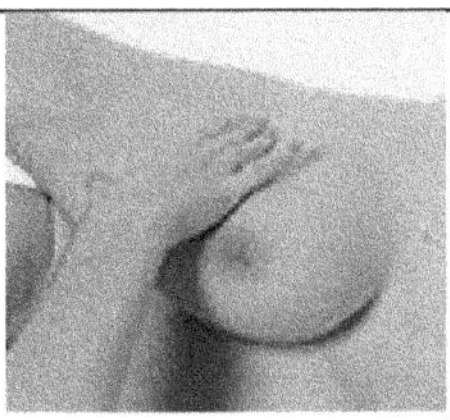 Lying on one side. Turning just enough to

feeling other breast.	make the breast move forward. Putting the back of hand of the side being checked on forehead.
Checking the outer half of the breast and up into the arm pit.	Checking the entire breast area. Swapping to feel other breast.

Breast Self Examination

Visual Field Examination

Suprasellar extension of a pituitary adenoma or other mass lesion may elevate and compress the optic chiasm, causing bitemporal hemianopia.

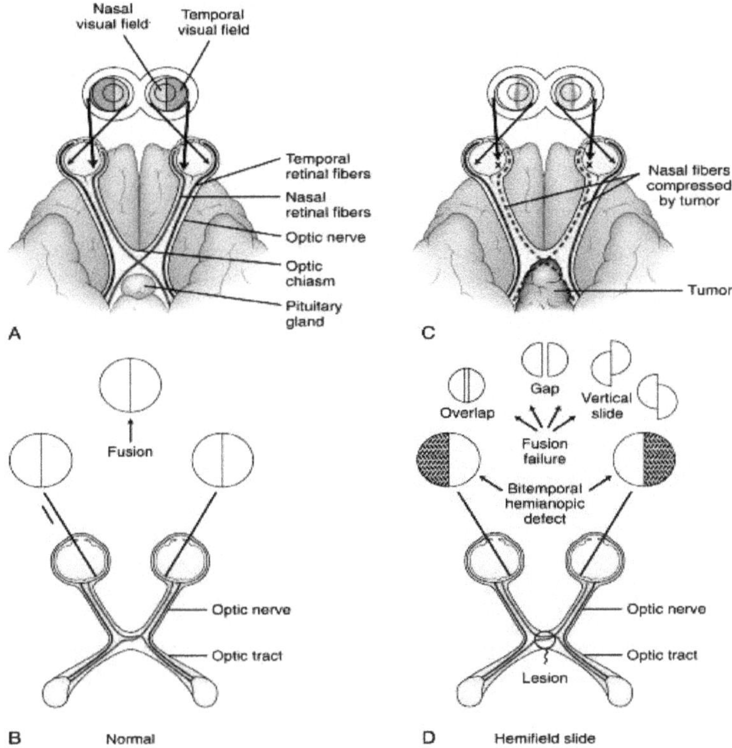

Local effects of an expanding pituitary tumor causing visual field defects

(A and B, Normal vision. C, Bitemporal hemianopia. D, Hemifield slide phenomena arising in the setting of bitemporal hemianopia from fusion instability. The nasal and temporal fields lose their linkage, resulting in overlap of the preserved visual fields

Asymmetrical involvement of the chiasm and optic nerves and tracts may produce different patterns of visual impairment. Clinical assessment of visual fields is difficult. All patients with suprasellar extension of a pituitary mass should undergo computerised (eg, Humphrey) assessment of visual fields.

Associated Signs-

Visual field defect, papilledoema, and cranial neuropathy suggest a pituitary tumor or an intracranial mass. The presence of goiter, coarse hair, dry skin, carotenemia, and myxedema indicates hypothyroidism. In contrast, the presence of goiter, hand tremor, and exophthalmos suggests thyrotoxicosis. Hirsutism and acne may be associated with chronic hyper-androgenism associated with hyperprolactinemia.

Laboratory Evaluation

Laboratory tests should be ordered only when indicated by the patient's history or physical examination. If there is doubt about the nature of the nipple discharge, Galactorrhoea can be confirmed by microscopic examination of the discharge for the presence of fat globules, or the discharge can be stained to detect fat.

Hormonal assey

If the diagnosis is not obvious, levels of serum prolactin, follicle-stimulating hormone, luteinizing hormone, and thyroid-stimulating hormone should be measured.

Because the secretion of prolactin is labile and episodic, an elevated prolactin level should be confirmed on at least two occasions when the patient is in a fasting, nonexercised state, with no breast stimulation. There is a direct correlation between the degree of hyperprolactinemia and the likelihood of finding a prolactin-secreting pituitary tumor. A serum prolactin level greater than 200 ng per mL (200 mcg per L) virtually assures the presence of a prolactinoma.

 Dr. Rajneesh Kumar Sharma

Macroprolactin test

Lab results indicating hyperprolactinemia need to be investigated for the presence of macroprolactin, a complex of Prolactin bound to IgG that has limited or no biological activity in the body. The most widely accepted method for differentiating macroprolactin from biologically active Prolactin is by precipitation

Pregnancy test

A pregnancy test should be considered for all postpubertal females. A beta-human chorionic gonadotropin test remains positive for weeks after termination of a pregnancy; it can be used to confirm a recent pregnancy.

Mammography

To exclude any tumor or neoplastic growth, mammography is necessary, especially in elderly.

Magnetic resonance imaging (MRI)

MRI of the pituitary fossa, preferably with gadolinium enhancement, should be considered if the serum prolactin level is significantly elevated or if a pituitary tumor is suspected. Computed tomography may not be sensitive enough to identify small lesions or large lesions that are isodense with surrounding structures. Patients with macroprolactinomas must be evaluated for hypopituitarism. Osteopenia and osteoporosis may be associated with hyperprolactinemia in children and adults as a result of estrogen inhibition in females and disturbances of vitamin D hydroxylation in both sexes. Bone densitometry should be considered if osteopenia or osteoporosis is suspected.

<u>Managementof Galactorrhoea</u>

Treatment of Galactorrhoea should be directed at the underlying cause. If possible, Galactorrhoea-inducing medications should be replaced with safe, alternative agents. Hypothyroidism should be treated with thyroid hormone replacement therapy. Self-manipulation of the breast should be stopped. Galactorrhoea secondary to maternal estrogen in infants is self-limited and does not require treatment. The decision to treat Galactorrhoea should be based on the serum prolactin level, severity of the Galactorrhoea, and the patient's fertility desires.

Allopathic Treatment of Galactorrhea

The management of galactorrhea typically involves the use of dopamine agonists, such as bromocriptine or cabergoline. These medications work by stimulating dopamine receptors in the brain, which in turn helps to normalize prolactin levels and reduce the size of prolactinomas (prolactin-secreting pituitary tumors).

- **Dopamine Agonists:** Drugs like bromocriptine and cabergoline are the mainstay of treatment for galactorrhea caused by hyperprolactinemia. They are effective in lowering prolactin levels and can lead to the shrinkage of prolactinomas, thereby alleviating symptoms of galactorrhea.
- **Surgical Intervention:** In cases where dopamine agonists are ineffective or poorly tolerated, surgical removal of the prolactinoma may be considered. This surgical approach is often followed by radiation therapy to prevent tumor recurrence.

- **Sex Steroid Replacement:** For individuals experiencing hormonal imbalances along with galactorrhea, replacement therapy with sex steroids may be necessary to restore normal reproductive function and menstrual cycles.
- **Treatment of Underlying Causes:** The treatment approach also involves addressing any underlying medical conditions that may be contributing to galactorrhea. For instance, if galactorrhea is secondary to hypothyroidism or medication side effects, treating the underlying cause is essential for resolving galactorrhea.

The choice of treatment depends on the specific cause of galactorrhea, the characteristics of the underlying tumor (if present), and individual patient factors. A comprehensive evaluation by endocrinologists, neurosurgeons, and reproductive specialists is often necessary to tailor treatment to each patient's needs and optimize outcomes.

Homoeopathic Treatment

Whatever the diagnosis may be, homoeopathic treatment is not dependent on it but causative entity should immediately be removed if possible. Homoeopathy considers person as a whole and the treatment is miraculously responsive. The homoeopathic treatment of Galactorrhoea can only be studied after one has thoroughly aqcuained the theory and philosophy of homoeopathy. This is described in further chapters in quite detail.

<u>Related conditions with 'Galactorrhoea'</u>

These are hyperprolactinemia, Gynaecomastia and Prolactinoma which should also be studied.

1- Hyperprolactinemia

Hyperprolactinemia is a condition characterized by elevated serum levels of the hormone. Prolactin in nonpregnant individuals. It occurs in both genders, although it is most prevalent among reproductive-aged women.

Aetiology

The main causes of hyperprolactinemia are pituitary tumors, primary hypothyroidism, hypothalamic disease, chronic kidney failure, cirrhosis and ingestion of drugs that block the Prolactin-inhibitory effects of dopamine such as tranquilizers, some hypertension medications and prescriptions for gastroesophageal reflux or nausea. Spinal cord damage and chest wall injury have also been shown to trigger excess Prolactin secretion. Many cases of hyperprolactinemia are classified as idiopathic.

Symptoms of Hyperprolactinemia in Women:

- Irregular menstruation
- Infertility
- Loss of libido
- Headache
- Peripheral vision problems
- Mood changes/depression
- Galactorrhea (milk discharge from the breasts)
- Menopausal symptoms

Symptoms of Hyperprolactinemia in Men:

- Impotence
- Infertility
- Loss of libido
- Headache
- Peripheral vision problems
- Mood changes/depression
- Gynecomastia (enlargement of breast tissue in men)
- Signs of increased androgen levels

These symptoms can vary in severity and presentation, and not all individuals with hyperprolactinemia will experience all of these symptoms.

2- Gynaecomastia

Gynaecomastia is the excessive development of the male mammary glands, due mainly to ductal proliferation with periductal edema; frequently secondary to increased estrogen levels; but mild Gynaecomastia may occur in normal adolescence.

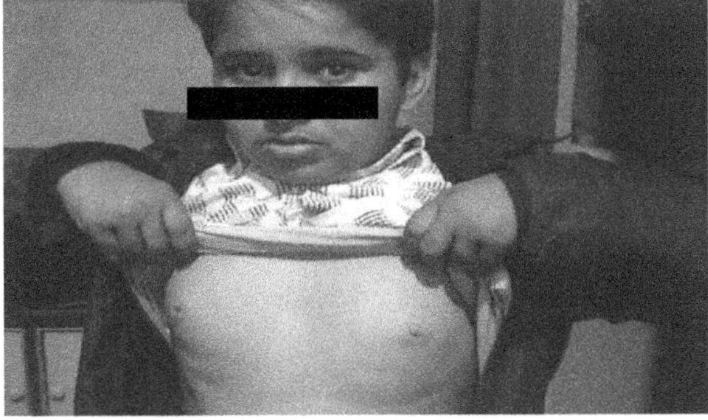

A Case of Gynecomastia
(From Case- file of HCRI)

It is the commonest condition affecting male breast and is due to enlargement of both ductal and stromal tissue. It is benign and often reversible usually presenting as uni or bilateral non-tender breast enlargement.

Aetiology

I. Idiopathic- Most cases are idiopathic.
II. Physiological- due to relative oestrogen excess i.e.
   a. Neonatal
   b. Puberty
   c. Senile
III. Pathologial causes
   a. Primary Testicular Failure
   b. Anorchia
   c. Klinefelter's Syndrome
   d. Bilateral Cryptorchidism
   e. Acquired Testicular Failure
   f. Mumps
   g. Irradiation
   h. Secondary Testicular Failure
   i. Generalised hypopituitarism
   j. Isolated gonadotrophin deficiency
   k. Endocrine Tumours
   l. Testicular
   m. Adrenal
   n. Pituitary
   o. Non-Endocrine Tumours
   p. Bronchial carcinoma
   q. Lymphoma
   r. Hypernephroma
   s. Hepatic Disease
   t. Cirrhosis
   u. Haemochromatosis

 Dr. Rajneesh Kumar Sharma

IV. Drugs
   a. Oestrogens and oestrogen agonists - digoxin, spironolactone
   b. hyperprolactinemia - methyldopa, phenothiazines
   c. Gonadotrophins
   d. Testosterone target cell inhibitors - cimetidine, cyproterone Acetate

3- Prolactinoma

Prolactinomas retain their responsiveness to the inhibitory effects of dopamine; therefore, their origin still remains somewhat vague.
Hypotheses include-
   a. Reduced dopamine concentrations in the pituitary portal system and
   b. Vascular isolation of the tumor which prevents dopamine inhibition.

Origin and structure of prolactinoma

These tumors originate in the lateral aspects of the anterior pituitary and are surrounded by a pseudo capsule. These tumors may be cystic or degenerating and are often discolored (blue, brown, or gray) as the result of hemorrhage.
The parenchymal cells of the tumors are densely arranged in small lobules which, in turn, are surrounded by abasement membrane. Secretary granules of Prolactin in these tumors are 400 to 500 nm in diameter, with normal lactotrophs containing 700 nm granules. Some have reported Prolactinomas in 12% to 25% of women with secondary amenorrhea; however, the actual incidence is somewhat less. The incidence of

Prolactinomas in women with 'Galactorrhoea' but regular menses is quite low.

Factors involved in pituitary tumor pathogenesis

- **Hereditary**

    o MEN-1
    o Transcription factor defect (e.g., Prop-1 excess)
    o Carney's complex
    o AIP mutation

- **Hypothalamic**

    o Excess GHRH or CRH production
    o Receptor activation
    o Dopamine deprivation

- **Pituitary**

    o Signal transduction mutations (e.g., gsp, CREB)
    o Disrupted paracrine growth factor or cytokine action (e.g., FGF-2, FGF-4, LIF, EGF, NGF)
    o Activated oncogene or cell cycle disruption (e.g., PTTG; ras; p27)
    o Intrapituitary paracrine hypothalamic hormone action (e.g., GHRH, TRH)
    o Loss of tumor suppressor gene function (11q13; 13)

- **Environmental**

    o Estrogens
    o Irradiation

- **Peripheral**

    o Target failure (ovary, thyroid, adrenal)
(CREB, cyclic adenosine monophosphate response

    Dr. Rajneesh Kumar Sharma

element–binding protein; CRH, corticotropin-releasing hormone; EGF, epidermal growth factor; FGF, fibroblast growth factor; GHRH, growth hormone–releasing hormone; LIF, leukemia growth factor; MEN-1, multiple endocrine neoplasia type 1; NGF, nerve growth factor; PTTG, pituitary tumor transforming gene; TRH, thyrotropin-releasing hormone)

Prevalence of Pituitary Adenoma by Type

- GH cell adenoma: 15%
- PRL cell adenoma: 30%
- GH and PRL cell adenoma: 7%
- ACTH cell adenoma: 10%
- Gonadotroph cell adenoma: 10%
- Nonfunctioning adenoma: 25%
- TSH cell adenoma: 1%
- Unclassified adenoma: 2%

Abbreviations:

- ACTH = Adrenocorticotropic hormone
- GH = Growth hormone
- PRL = Prolactin
- TSH = Thyroid-stimulating hormone

Signs of Pituitary Tumors Secondary to Mass Effect

- Headache
- Chiasmal syndrome
- Hypothalamic syndrome
- Disturbances of thirst, appetite, satiety, sleep, and temperature
- Diabetes insipidus

- • Syndrome of inappropriate ADH secretion (SIADH)
- • Obstructive hydrocephalus
- • Cranial nerves III, IV, V1, V2, and VI dysfunction
- • Frontal and temporal lobe syndromes
- • Cerebrospinal fluid Rhinorrhea

These signs can vary based on the size and location of the pituitary tumor and its impact on surrounding structures.

Local effects of an expanding pituitary or hypothalamic mass

- **Pituitary**

  - o Adult hyposomatotrophism
  - o Growth failure
  - o Hypoadrenalism
  - o Hypogonadism
  - o Hypothyroidism

- **Optic tract**

  - o Bitemporal hemianopia
  - o Blindness
  - o Loss of red perception
  - o Scotoma
  - o Superior or bitemporal field defect

- **Hypothalamus**

  - o Appetite, behavioral, and autonomic nervous system dysfunctions
  - o Temperature dysregulation, obesity, diabetes insipidus

- o Thirst, sleep

- **Cavernous sinus**

  - o Diplopia
  - o Facial numbness
  - o Ophthalmoplegia
  - o Ptosis

- **Temporal lobe**

  - o Uncinate seizures

- **Frontal lobe**

  - o Anosmia
  - o Personality disorder

- **Central**

  - o Dementia
  - o Headache
  - o Hydrocephalus
  - o Laughing seizures
  - o Psychosis

- **Neuro-ophthalmologic tract**

  - o **Field Defects**

    - Bitemporal hemianopia (50%), amaurosis with hemianopia (12%), contralateral or monocular hemianopia (7%)

  - o **Homonymous hemianopia**

    - Scotomas: Hemianopic; junctional; monocular central, arcuate, altitudinal

  - o **Acuity Loss**

    - Color vision

- Contrast sensitivity
- Snellen
- Visual evoked potential

- **Pupillary Abnormality**

  - Afferent defect
  - Impaired light reactivity

- **Optic Atrophy**

  - Cranial nerve palsy: Abducens, oculomotor, sensory trigeminal, trochlear
  - Nystagmus
  - Papilledema
  - Postfixation blindness
  - Visual hallucinations

The pituitary tumors of less than 10 mm size are called microadenoma and larger ones as macroadenoma.

Microadenoma

A pituitary microadenoma or hyperplasia is the cause of hyperprolactinemia in most patients. In over one-third of women with hyperprolactinemia, a radiologic abnormality consistent with an adenoma is found. In the remainder, simple hyperplasia of the pituitary lactotrophs is assumed to be the cause. Most of these abnormalities are microadenomas (< 1 cm), and patients can generally be reassured of a benign course of disease. Hypotheses for the formation of microadenomas and macroadenomas (> 1 cm) include are reduction in dopamine concentrations in the hypophyseal portal system, vascular isolation of the tumor, or both.

The tumors, which originate in the lateral aspects of the anterior pituitary, are surrounded by a pseudo capsule.

They may be cystic or degenerating and are often discolored (blue, gray or brown) as a result of hemorrhage.

Treatment

Microadenomas rarely progress to macroadenomas. Therapies include expectant, medical and/or rarely surgical therapy. All women are advised to notify their physician of chronic headaches, visual disturbances (particularly tunnel vision consistent with bitemporal hemianopsia), and extraocular muscle palsies. Formal visual field testing is rarely necessary. Under homoeopathic treatment, these are frequently curable.

AllopathicTreatment

Ergot alkaloids are the mainstay of therapy. Bromocriptine is used to treat hyperprolactinemia caused by a pituitary adenoma. The ergot alkaloids increase dopamine levels, thus decreasing Prolactin levels. The serum half-life is 3.5 hours, and twice-a-day administration is required. Ergot alkaloids are excreted via the biliary tree; therefore, caution is required in the presence of liver disease. The major adverse effects include nausea, headaches, hypotension, dizziness, fatigue and drowsiness, vomiting, headaches, nasal congestion, and constipation. Many patients tolerate the drug on the following regimen: one-half tablet every evening (1.25 mg) at bedtime for one week, an increase of one-half tablet every evening in the second week, and every morning in the third week, and finally 2.5 mg twice a day. The lowest dose that maintains the Prolactin level in the normal range is continued. An alternative to oral administration is the vaginal administration of bromocriptine tablets, which is well tolerated. When cannot be used, other medications such as pergolide, cabergoline, metergoline may be used. In patients with a microadenoma who are receiving bromocriptine therapy, a repeat MRI scan may be performed at 6 to 12 months after Prolactin levels are normal. Normal Prolactin levels and resumption of menses should not be considered proof of tumor response to treatment.

Further MRI scans should be performed only to evaluate new symptoms. Discontinuation of bromocriptine therapy after two to three years may be attempted because some adenomas undergo hemorrhagic necrosis and cease to function. Further attempted, as some adenomas undergo hemorrhagic necrosis and cease to function.

Macroadenomas

Macroadenomas are pituitary tumors greater than 1 cm in size. Evaluation for other trophic hormone deficiencies may be indicated.

Macroadenoma symptoms include severe headaches, visual field changes, and rarely, diabetes insipidus and blindness. After Prolactin has reached normal levels, a follow-up MRI is indicated within six months to document shrinkage or stabilization of growth. This may be performed earlier if symptoms develop or exacerbate. Normalized Prolactin levels or resumption of menses should not be taken as proof of tumor response to treatment.

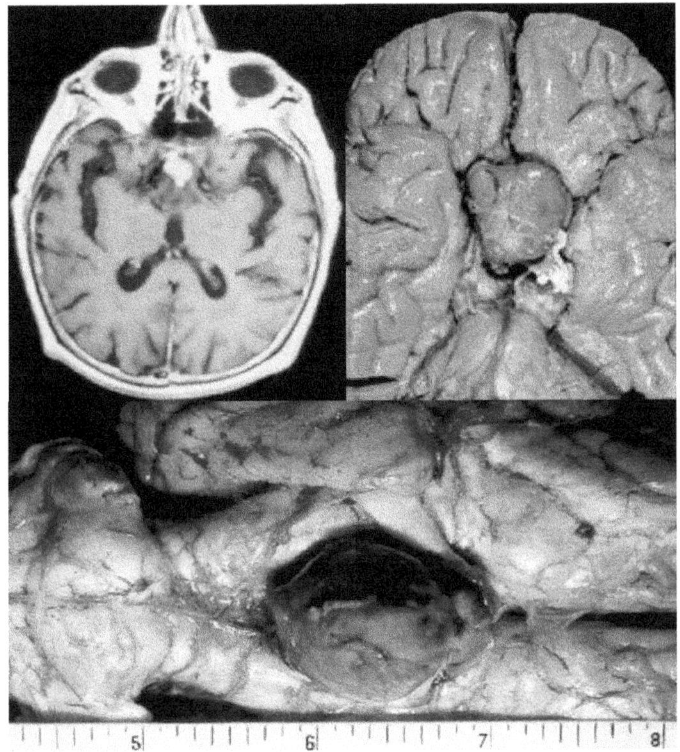

Ptuitary Adenoma- CT and gross appearance

Allopathic Treatment

Macroadenomas treated with bromocriptine routinely show a decrease in Prolactin levels and size; nearly one-half show a 50% reduction in size and another one-fourth show a 33% reduction after six months of therapy. Tumor re-growth occurs in over 60% of cases after discontinuation of bromocriptine therapy; therefore, long-term therapy is the rule.

After stabilization of tumor size is documented, the MRI scan is repeated six months later and, if stable, yearly for several years. Serum Prolactin levels are measured every six months. Because tumors may enlarge despite normalized Prolactin values, re-evaluation of symptoms at regular intervals (six months) is required.

Surgical Intervention

Tumors that are unresponsive to bromocriptine or that cause persistent visual field loss require surgical intervention. Unfortunately, despite surgical resection, recurrences of hyperprolactinemia and tumor growth are not uncommon. Complications of surgery include cerebral carotid artery injury, diabetes insipidus, meningitis, nasal septal perforation, partial or pan hypopituitarism, spinal fluid rhinorrhea, third nerve palsy, and recurrence. Pre treatment with bromocriptine may result in fibrosis, making resection more difficult. Periodic MRI scanning after surgery is indicated, particularly in patients with recurrent hyperprolactinemia.

Transphenoidal surgery achieves resolution of hyperprolactinemia with resumption of menses in 40% with macroadenomas, and 80% with microadenomas. Recurrence after surgery is approximately 50% (range 10% to 70%). Unfortunately, 10% to 30% of patients undergoing surgery develop panhypopituitarism. Other problems of surgery include CSF leaks, meningitis, and frequent diabetes insipidus after surgery.

Other Considerations in the Treatment of Pituitary Adenomas

Recent studies and autopsy surveys indicate that estrogen administration is not associated with clinical, biochemical, or radiological evidence of growth of

   Dr. Rajneesh Kumar Sharma

pituitary microadenomas or the progression of idiopathic hyperprolactinemia to an adenoma status. For these reasons, estrogen replacement or oral contraceptive use for hypo estrogenic hyperprolactinemic patients secondary to microadenoma or hyperplasia is appropriate.

Pituitary Adenomas in Pregnancy

Prolactin-secreting microadenomas rarely create complications during pregnancy. However, monitoring of patients with serial gross visual field examinations and fundoscopic examination is recommended. If persistent headaches, visual field deficits, or visual or fundoscopic changes occur, MRI scanning is advisable. Because serum Prolactin levels are elevated throughout pregnancy, Prolactin measurements are of no value. Although not recommended, bromocriptine use during pregnancy in women with symptomatic (visual field defects, headaches) microadenoma enlargement has resulted in resolution of deficits and symptoms. Women with previous transsphenoidal hypophysectomy and macroadenomas are monitored, as are those with microadenomas, with the addition of monthly Goldman perimetry visual field testing. Periodic MRI scanning may be necessary in women with symptoms or visual changes. Bromocriptine has been used on a temporary basis to resolve symptoms and visual field deficits in symptomatic macroadenoma patients to allow completion of pregnancy before initiation of definitive therapy. Breast feeding is not contraindicated in the presence of microadenomas or macroadenomas.

An overview of Galactorrhoea

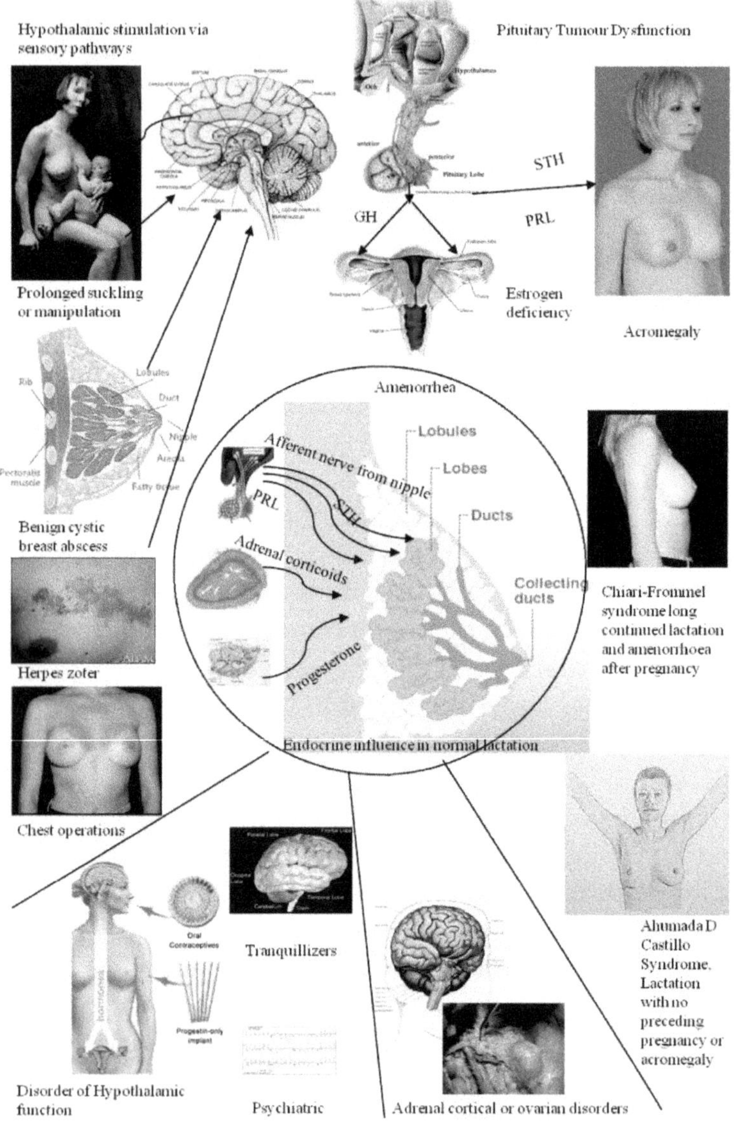

Dr. Rajneesh Kumar Sharma

<u>Homoeopathic Treatment</u>

To study Homoeopathic treatment of these conditions, one must we well contented with study of fundamentals of homoeopathy. The next chapters will describe homoeopathy in brief and the homoepathic treatment for all these conditions in detail.

Homoeopathy- A Breif Study

Concepts and Principles

Homoeopathy is the system of treatment based on demonstrable laws and principles, which are -

The Law of Similars-

It is also called the Law of Cure. This law demonstrates that the selected remedy is able to produce a range of symptoms in a healthy person similar to that observed in the patient, thus leading to the principle of Similia Similibus Curentur i.e. let likes be treated by likes. To give a simple example the effects of peeling an onion are very similar to the symptoms of acute cold. The remedy prepared from the bitch's milk, Lac caninum, is used to treat the Galactorrhoea in which the symptoms resemble those we get from taking it in potentized form in healthy state.

The Law of Single Remedy-

This law directs to choose and administer such a single remedy, which is most similar to the symptom complex of the sick person at a time.

The Law of Minimum Dose-

The similar remedy selected for a sick should be prescribed in minimum dose, so that when administered there is no toxic effects on the body. It just acts as a triggering and catalytic agent; to stimulate and strengthen the existing defense mechanism of the body. It does not need to be repeated frequently.

Holistic approach and Theory of Individualisation

This is a key point and unique to Homoeopathy. Even though it may sound strange, Homoeopathy does not treat disease per se. A Homoeopath does not concentrate his therapy on, say Galactorrhoea or prolactinoma or gyanecomastia. In other words he does not limit his treatment to overflowing milk from the breasts, macroadenoma or a infertility. Rather, he treats all aspects mental, emotional and physical of the person who happens to be suffering with Galactorrhoea or prolactinoma or gyanecomastia.
Homoeopathy regards each patient as a unique individual, e.g. six persons with Galactorrhoea might get a different Homoeopathic remedy, each one aimed at the individual's totality of symptoms rather than at his liver alone. The physicians' interest is not only to alleviate the patients' present symptoms but also his long-term well being.

Concept of Vital Force

This vital force is the dynamic, imponderable, invisible universal force of life energy found in all the living and to some extent in nonliving things also. One can easily appreciate its presence in living things due to visible results. Its existence in nonliving things can only be explained by science.
Every thing consists of small units of molecules. These molecules are made of tiny atoms. Each atom is made of

electrons, protons and neutrons (now presence of some more constituents has been proved viz. Positron etc.). Most of these finest particles are electrically charged and are kept together by electromagnetic field of attraction. These ultimate constituents are in the state of certain rhythmical and precise motions, and consequently, whole structure is in a state of harmonious oscillations and vibrations.

Great scientist Albert Einstein says —

'MASS' and 'ENERGY' are inter-convertible. The ultimate result of divisions of a substance is energy. Whenever anything is tried to divide a matter beyond atomic state, nothing is left except energy, in the form of photons. This energy is nothing but a form of life energy, equivalent to vital force.

Thus, this energy or vital force is omnipresent and is infinte. Everything uses a very little fraction of this force to exist.

Hahnemann Says-

"In the healthy condition of man, the spiritual vital force (autocracy), the dynamis that animates the material body (organism), rules with unbounded sway, and retains all the parts of the organism in admirable, harmonious, vital operation, as regards both sensations and functions, so that our indwelling, reason-gifted mind can freely employ this living, healthy instrument for the higher purposes of our existence". (Aphorism no. 9)

According to Dr. Kent the Vital Force or the simple substance has the character of formative intelligence, is subject to changes, pervades the material substance without replacing it, creating order in the body, belonging to the realm of quantity (the realms of degrees of fineness) being adaptable and being constructive.

To sum up the idea of Vital Force as presented by Dr. Kent is given above, according to Dr. Vithoulkas it is the defence mechanism in the living body and according to the ancient Indian thought it is the sookshama shareera (the subtle body) or the consciousness.

Experience has well established the fact that the innerself of the living organism governs. When this innerself is disordered, as seen during diseases, whole being gets disordered. This disordered state is represented by various signs and symptoms, if these signs and symptoms are not interpreted properly in the beginning of the disease and not remedied by proper homoeopathic medicines, gross irreversible pathological changes take place and recovery becomes more and more tedious or impossible.

Similarly, the drugs when potentized and proved well, become live entities and capable of affecting the innerself instantly.

Chronic Diseases-

Hahnemann observed that the acute diseases were cured successfully but the constitional health of the patients was not improving, rather declining. He quietly searched for the fundamental cause of the chronic diseases that was slowly destroying the health of the patients. The outcome of this research was published in 1828 in the first edition of his great work, The Chronic Diseases Their Peculiar Nature and their Homoeopathic Cure, commonly known as The Chronic Diseases.

 Dr. Rajneesh Kumar Sharma

By "Chronic Disease" Dr. Hahnemann did not mean exactly the same thing as is now generally understood by the phrase - a disease that lasts a long time and is incurable. To make his meaning clear, I can not do better than quote Dr. Hahnemann's own definition of acute and chronic diseases, from paragraph 72 of his Organon:

"The diseases to which is liable are either rapid morbid processes of the abnormally deranged vital force, which have a tendency to finish their course more or less quickly, but always in a moderate time - these are termed acute diseases; or they are diseases of such a character that, with small, often imperceptible beginnings, dynamically derange the living organism, each in its own peculiar manner, and cause it to deviate from the healthy condition in such a way that the automatic life energy, called vital force, whose office it is preserve the health, only opposes to them at the commencement and during their progress, imperfect, unsuitable, useless resistance, but must helplessly suffer (them to spread and) itself to be more and more abnormally deranged, until at length the organism is destroyed; these are termed chronic diseases. They are caused by infection from a chronic miasm."

Miasm-

Ancient Greek physician, Hippocrates, taught that all diseases were caused by the predisposition inherent in the innate constitution and its susceptibility to a constellation of causation rather than any one single effect. In the Greek philosophy disease is caused by an interdependent set of circumstances which disrupts the natural ebb and flow of the pneuma (vital force) within the organism.

In his Organon of Medicine, Samuel Hahnemann
separated the origin of disease into two categories, the
exciting and fundamental causes, and related them very
closely to the susceptibility of the physical constitution.
It is necessary for a homoeopath to understand the
nature of the exciting causes of acute diseases as well as
the underlying fundamental cause of long lasting
diseases, which is usually due to the chronic miasms.
Acute diseases are self-limiting disorders which have
quick onsets, rapid progressions, and a tendency to
develop an immediate crisis. Many of these acute
diseases are actually acute acerbations of the chronic
states latent within the constitution that have been
brought forth by exciting factors. The nature of chronic
miasmic disease is slow and insidious in its onset and
gradual in its progression. These negative
transformations gradually increase until they bring on
complex pathologies that eventually are the cause of
premature old age and death. The chronic miasms are
the effects of infections that are non self-limiting which
cause considerable damage to the immune system, the
vital force, and the constitution.

Hahnemann taught that the susceptibility to the
exciting factors lies in the fundamental cause which is
attributed to the chronic miasms. The etiology of a
disease, the constitution and temperament of the
individual, and the totality of the signs and symptoms
are three factors that form a complete picture of an
illness.

In Homoeopathy we often speak of the totality of the
symptoms as the basis of selecting a remedy, but
sometimes we forget to include the causative factors,

the miasms, and the nature of the physical constitution of the individual. Understanding the innate constitution is fundamental to homoeopathic treatment because it holds the keys to an individual's susceptibility as well as the inherited effects of the chronic miasms. Hippocrates was the first physician to use the term "miasm" which has its origins in the Greek word for taint or fault. He postulated that certain infectious diseases were transmitted to humans by air and water tainted by miasms. In late 18th century it was a common belief that miasms were impure airs that were responsible for the spread of epidemic diseases among groups of people. Hahnemann realized that the air could carry infectious diseases but he did not consider the pathogenic material to be gaseous in nature. By the late 1790s Hahnemann had realized that syphilis was an infectious blood disease that could mask itself with the symptoms of many different illnesses. Early in his career he made a special preparation called Mercurius Solubilis Hahnemanni that was the standard treatment for syphilis throughout Europe. He soon found that Mercury in homoeopathic potency worked much better on syphilis than the crude poisonous form and he recorded several permanent cures.

A Dutch naturalist named van Leeuwenhoek invented the microscope and published his observations of small living "animalcules" before in his death in 1723. This information led Hahnemann to believe that microorganisms were at the root of many infectious diseases. For this reason he supported the ideas of the animalculists but at the same time upheld the importance of susceptibility of the host constitution. Very early in his career Hahnemann suggested that certain skin eruptions, such as "crusta lactea", were being caused by microscopic "miasmic animalcule" i.e., micro-organisms. At this time there were four major theories about diseases that spread in an infectious manner.

- Miasma as a foul gaseous exhalation.
- The theory of the animalcule.
- The zymotic theory.
- The theory of spontaneous generation.

Some scientists suggested that certain substances called "zymes" that were inert outside the body could lie dormant until the internal terrain made it possible for them to multiply and caused specific diseases. The observations of the zymotists are very similar to the activities of viral material in the human body. The term zymotic can be found in the old homoeopathic literature and is a rubric in the general section of Kent's Repertory. Hahnemann synthesized the ideas of the animalcule and zymes and redefined the Hippocratic term "miasma" to express the constitutional derangements caused by parasitic infections. He carefully separated the self-limiting acute miasms from the syndromes of long lasting diseases and started to develop a special materia medica and repertory for the treatment of the chronic miasms. Therefore, in Hahnemannian Homoeopathy the word "miasm" means the effects of microorganisms on the vital force including the symptoms that are transmitted to the following generations. These chronic miasms are capable of producing degenerative illnesses, auto-immune diseases and lead the organism toward immuno-deficiency disorders.

Phases of Miasms-

Hahnemann noticed that each of the chronic diseases has three phases-
- Primary stage
- Latent stage
- Secondary or tertiary state.

The effects of these miasms were then passed from one generation to the next generation by inheritance and caused predispositions to certain disease syndromes. In condition of Galactorrhoea, all the miasms frequently show their active part and according to their sequence of activity, the whole process of Galactorrhoea is settled.

Types of Miasms-

The three chronic miasms that Hahnemann introduced in 1828 were called-
- Psora (the itch miasm)
- Sycosis (the gonorrheal miasm)
- Syphilis (the chancre miasm).

From the time of Hippocrates healers conjectured about the possibility of invisible organisms causing disease but Hahnemann founded the modern concept of infection. In the preface of Charles Hempel's translation of the Organon, Constantine Hering recorded that late in his life Hahnemann made further discoveries and developed a new aspect of the theory of Psora with the introduction of a new miasm he called Pseudo-psora. Hering wrote:

"Hahnemann distinguishes the venereal miasms as syphilis and sycosis; and also subdivides psora with pseudo- Hahnemann's miasmic theory now contained two venereal and two non-venereal miasms that produced life-long chronic diseases. The two non-venereal miasms are Psora (the itch disease) and Pseudo-psora (the tubercle disease). The two venereal miasms are Sycosis (the fig wart diseases) and Syphilis (the chancre disease). Hahnemann noticed that some cases that appeared to be Psora did not depend exclusively on an external skin eruption for their development. He observed that this disease was infectious in nature and possessed primary, latent, and secondary symptoms as well as inherited aspects. He decided that it was caused by a miasmic agent with a distinct etiology so he separated its symptoms from Psora and made a new classification called the Pseudo-psora, the TB miasm. All of these miasms may be acquired through a primary infection or their effects can be experienced through heredity.

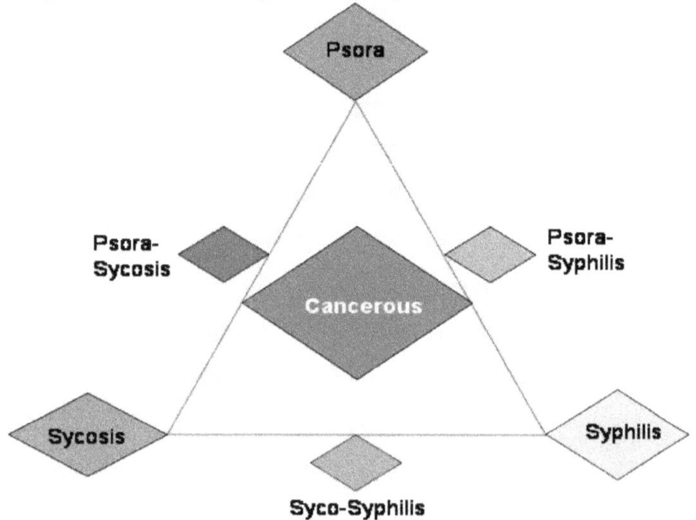

The Fundamental Miasms and Their Combinations

   Dr. Rajneesh Kumar Sharma

It is sometimes considered, if Hahnemann taught that all long-lasting diseases are caused by chronic miasms. This is not the total picture. In the Organon, he mentions three classifications of long lasting disease:

- Those caused by continuing stress factors (disorders upheld by maintaining causes which by their nature are not necessarily true chronic disorders §73),
- Those caused by drug toxicity and faulty treatment (physician caused §74.),
- Those caused by infectious miasms (naturally caused §78).

Signs and Symptoms of Miasms-

Each of the chronic miasms have their own characteristic signs that are an integral part of the totality of the symptoms. For example-

- Psora tends to produce irritation, inflammation, and hypersensitivity.
- Sycosis tends to produce infiltrations, indurations, and over growth.
- Pseudo-psora tends toward tubercles, fibrosis and suppuration.
- Syphilis tends toward granulation, degeneration and ulceration.

Physical constitution-

- Psora tends to make the organism toxic, the skin unhealthy, and perverts the functions of the digestive and eliminative organs.
- Pseudo-psora tends to produce pipe stem bones, narrow chests, sunken cheeks and sparkling eyes.
- Sycosis tends to cause heavy bones, water

retention, over growth of tissue like gynaecomastia, hirsutism and slow metabolism.

- Syphilis tends to cause congenital defects, asymmetrical bony structure, deformed teeth and the classic bull dog face.

Temperament-

- Psora is full of pseudo-scientific, philosophical, political, religious ideas. They are self expressive, talkative, self deceptive and may think they are full of genius yet seem foolish and impractical to others.
- Pseudo-psora (Tubercular miasm) is romantic, erotic, social, extroverted, cosmopolitan, erratic, optimistic, yet dissatisfied and always wants to change places, jobs, mates, etc.
- Sycosis is pessimistic, a hard realist, skeptical, secretive, suspicious, jealous and has fixed ideas and hidden self disgust.
- Syphilis has a mixture of madness and genius with a deep sense of irony that leads to obsession with death and destruction. They become guilty, self destructive, and end in idiocy, insanity or suicide.

Pains-

- Psora pains are itchy, crawling, tickling, and burning
- Pseudo-psora pains are neuralgic, sharp, piercing, twisting, stitching.
- Sycosis pains are sudden, intense, spasmodic, crampy and colicky.
- Syphilis pains are lacking for the condition present or are deep, aching, agonizing, and esp. < at night.

Discharges-

- Psora has fairly scanty, irritating, itchy discharges.
- Pseudo-psora has pussy, purulent, yellow, bloody, musty discharges.
- Sycosis has pungent, brine-like, fishy odors with watery greenish or dirty brown discharges.
- Syphilitic miasm has very offensive, foul, putrid, smelly discharges.

Skin-

- Psora is dry, rough, unhealthy, every little injury becomes infected and the lesions are itchy and have scanty pus. The symptoms repeatedly found with Galactorrhoea cases.
- Pseudo-psora is translucent, fine, smooth, bruises easily, and its lesions bleed easily and exude excessive pus.
- Sycosis is full of warts, flecks, moles, growths, dark discolorations with over growth of hair- so called hirsutism.
- Syphilitic skin has brownish red, or coppery color spots, eruptions that do not itch, and a tendency toward easy ulceration.

The final combination of all the three miasms is called cancerous miasm and produces the worst forms of illness viz. tumours like prolactinoma, micro or macroadenoma etc.

Thus we can see that in Dr. Hahnemann's method the totality of the symptoms includes the signs and symptoms of the miasms classified by their layers and listed according to their development. The active miasm is the center on which the totality of symptoms is built so that the remedy chosen matches the underlying miasm syndromes.

Dr. Allen offered his opinion as to the use of the totality without an understanding of the chronic miasms and their layers in his classic, The Chronic Miasms.

"I think I hear many say, are not the totality of the symptoms, all there is to disease? Yes, but to me it is necessary to know something of what is behind that grouping of the totality. If you do not know this you are prescribing for a Jack-in-the-box. You cannot follow the evolution of the curative process; you cannot even prescribe intelligently the proper diet for a patient, unless you know the basic miasm. Of course the diseases that are present will help you to some extent, but you have no surety unless you know the underlying basic disturber of the disordered life".

Totality, Constitution and the Miasms-

The etiology of a disease, the constitutional temperament of the patient, and the totality of the signs and symptoms are three factors that form a complete picture of a disease. In Homoeopathy we often speak of the totality of the symptoms as the basis of selecting a remedy, but sometimes we forget to include the causative factors, miasms, and the physical constitution of the individual. The physical signs of a person are fundamental to the treatment of chronic disorders because the constitution and temperament shows the effects of the inherited miasms.

We must get beyond relying solely on the personal or family history to uncover miasms. The miasms are present in the very symptomatology of the client. The syndromes produced by the miasms point to the fundamental cause even if it can not be traced in the case taking to a specific etiologic factor. In this way, to treat a seemingly simple case of Galactorrhoea, it is neccessory to collect all the signs and symptoms to constitute the totality for correct treatment.

Idiosyncracy

No two individuals are alike. They differ from each other in several ways viz. mental, physical, social, pathological or their responces to the external stimuli. The most important becomes the susceptibility of the individual which ascertains his inclination to be sick or to be extraordinarily susceptible to certain things for which other persons are not normally reactant or too responsive. In modern terminology the term idiosyncracy has been replaced with allergy and the various stimuli are termed as allergens. This condition of being hypersensititive for certain stimuli, either external or internal, is called idiosyncracy. Idiosyncratics are more susceptible to various causes and more prone to have Galactorrhoea.

Indisposition

Often, the stimuli affecting an individual may disturb his normal health economy slightly and temporarily, which almost always autoreversible. This condition of slight deviation from health is called indisposition which usually requires no medical treatment and is spontaneously recovered. Very frequently, we see the cases of idiopathic Galactorrhoea, which fall in this category. By slight correction in habit, habitat and dietary regimen and removal of exciting cause, the condition may be cured completely.

'Galactorrhoea' and Homoeopathy

Sign or Symptom	Fundamental Miasm	Secondary/ Associated Miasm
Normal Lactation Increased	Psora	
Lactation Increased considerably	Sycosis	Psora
Amenorrhoea	Psora	Syphilis
Irregular Menses	Psora	
Infertility	Psora	Syphilis, Sycosis
Loss of Libido	Syphilis	Psora
Headache	Psora	Syphilis, Sycosis
Peripheral Vision Changes	Psora	Syphilis, Sycosis
Mood Changes	Psora	
Depression	Syphilis	Psora
Menopausal Symptoms in spite of normal or elevated Oestrogen Levels	Sycosis	
Corpus Leutium Dysfunction	Psora	Syphilis
Androgens Elevation	Sycosis	Psora
Gynaecomastia	Sycosis	Psora

Miasmatic Analysis of Signs and Symptoms associated with 'Galactorrhoea'

Prognosis of Galactorrhoea in Homoeopathic View

In a study of Galactorrhoea, the role of Homoeopathy in its treatment was analysed. The mode of prescription in various cases was based on totality of symptoms. The way to reach the similimum remedy was either through mental to physical generals and particulars; or through the key of rare and peculier symptoms if available in some cases.

The following results were obtained-

Gross Cure incidence

The Homoeopathic treatment was found to be miraculously effective in treatment of Galactorrhoea. The data revealed- Cured- 73 %, Relieved- 09 % and Not Cured- only 18 % .

Cure incidence based on Socioeconomic Status

The cure rate was highest in middle class patients and the lowest in poors.

Cure incidence based on Menstrual states

Females with normal menses were 70% cured those with scanty menses were 100% cured, those with amenorrhoea were 69% cured and postmenopausal ones were 100% cured.

Cure incidence based on Miasms

The highiest percentage of cure was in Pseudopsora (100%) and the least in Sycosis (00%). Psora was cured 79% and Psora- sycosis (50%) with 38% relief.

Remedial incidence in Galactorrhoea cases

The following remedies were found frequently in

repertorizations and percentage is given according to the number of cases the remedy is utilized.

- Lycopodium- 18%
- Phosphorus- 15%
- Conium, Lac- caninum Thuja and Tuberculinum- 12%
- Nat mur- 09%
- Acid nit, Ars alb, Bacil, Calc carb, Carcin, Ign, Med, Puls- 06%
- Arg nit, Bry, Caust, Cup m, Ginkgo b, Iod, Kali s, Kreos, Lac cap, Merc sol, Petrol, Podo, Sabal s, Sep, and Zinc- 03%

While looking at percentage of cure follwing results were obtained

Bacillinum, Causticum, Ginkgo bil, Iodium, Lac can, Lac caprinum, Merc sol, Podophyllum, Psorinum, Sabal-ser and Zinc met were rarely used and there percentage of cure was 100%.

- Lycopodium had cure rate of 67%
- Conium- 50%
- Thuja- 50%
- Tuberculinum- 50%
- Phosphorus- 40%

Literature related with 'Galactorrhoea' found in various Homoeopathic Books-

THERAPEUTICS

1. Allen, H. C. – Materia Medical of some important Nosodes
> Publisher's Preface
> Ustilago maydis
> **Pregnancy, Parturition, Lactation**
- Agalactia; chronic inflammation, and indurations of mamma.
  - 'Galactorrhoea'.

2. Blackwood, A. – A Manual of Materia Medica, Therapeutics and Pharmacology
> Materia Medica
> Salvia officinalis
> **Therapeutics**
- It is useful in "Galactorrhoea".

3. Boericke, William – Pocket Manual of Homoeopathic Materia Medica
> Remedies
> Borax veneta
> **Female**
- 'Galactorrhoea'. [Cal.; Con.; Bell.] In nursing, pain in opposite breast.

4. Boericke, William – Pocket Manual of Homoeopathic Materia Medica
> Remedies
> Lac caninm
- 'Galactorrhoea'.

5. Boericke, William – Pocket Manual of Homoeopathic Materia Medica
> Remedies

Phytolacca decandra
Female
- Mastitis; mammae hard and very sensitive.
- Tumors of the breasts with enlarged axillary glands.
- Cancer of breast.
- Breast is hard, painful and of purple hue.
- Mammary abscess.
- Irritable breasts, before and during menses.
- 'Galactorrhoea'. [Calc.]

6. Boericke, William – Pocket Manual of Homoeopathic Materia Medica

Remedies
Salvia officinalis
- 'Galactorrhoea'.

7. Boger, C. M. – A Synoptic Key of the Materia Medica

Remedies
Lac caninm
Symptoms
- Breasts sore and swelled, before menses.
- 'Galactorrhoea'.
- DRIES UP THE MILK.
- Scanty milk.

8. Borland, D. M. - Homoeopathy for Mother and Infant

Remedies for Lactation
Lac caninum
- 'Galactorrhoea'.
- Or, loses milk while nursing.
- Serviceable in almost all cases were it is required to dry up milk. (ALUMEN, BELL.).

9. Borland, D. M. - Homoeopathy for Mother and

Dr. Rajneesh Kumar Sharma

Infant

Remedies for Lactation
Pulsatilla pretensis
- Milk thin and watery.
- Acrid milk.
- "Galactorrhoea" in women who are not nursing their children: but always in the gentle, tearful type of patients.
- After weaning, breasts swell, feel stretched and tense, intensely sore.
- Milk continues to be secreted.

10. Burt, W. H. – Physiological Materia Medica

Materia Medica
Iodium
Glandular system
- In such patients, prostatitis in the male, and amenorrhoea, "Galactorrhoea", and leucorrhoea in the female, subject, have been cured by it.

11. Burt, W. H. – Physiological Materia Medica

Materia Medica
Jaborandi
Sexual organs
Female
- In nursing women, where the secretion of milk has been very deficient, Dr. Bartholow has used the fluid extract with complete success; and Dr. Ringer has used it successfully in "Galactorrhoea".

12. Burt, W. H. – Physiological Materia Medica

Materia Medica
Phytolacca decandra
Sexual organs
Female

- Inflammation, swelling, and suppuration of the mammae.
- Mammae full of hard, painful nodosities.
- 'Galactorrhoea'; profuse discharge of milk; great exhaustion.
- Irritable mammae, (externally and internally); nursing very painful.
- This is one of our most useful drugs in many diseases of the mammae but it must be used locally as well as internally.
- Mastitis where the hardness is very apparent from the first; much sensitiveness.
  (See Belladonna, Conium, and Graphites.)
- Cancer of the mammae has (apparently) been cured many times with this drug.

13. Choudhury, N. M. - A Study on Materia Medica

Materia Medica

Calcarea carbonica

- It also becomes useful in various disorders, relating to secretion of milk after child-birth.
- It is almost like a panacea in all such disorders, arising out of excessive or deficient secretion of milk.
- It checks "Galactorrhoea" as well as helps to remove scantiness of the flow of milk.
- It goes even further, and improves the quality of the mother's milk.

14. Clarke J. H. - Dictionary of Practical Materia Medica

Remedies

Conium maculatum

Clinical

- 'Galactorrhoea'.

15. Clarke J. H. Dictionary of Practical Materia Medica

Remedies

Iodum

Clinical

- 'Galactorrhoea'. goŒtre.

16. Clarke J. H. - Dictionary of Practical Materia Medica

Remedies

Iodium

Symptoms

Female Sexual Organs

- 'Galactorrhoea'; thin, watery milk; weakness; emaciation.
- Milk suppressed; breasts atrophied and relaxed.

17. Clarke J. H. - Dictionary of Practical Materia Medica

Remedies

Lac caninum

Symptoms

Female Sexual Organs

- Breasts very sore and sensitive to pressure for a day or two during menses.
- Breasts very sore and painful, with sharp, darting pain in right ovarian region extending to knee, very painful and must keep leg flexed (1st d. after miscarriage at 6th month).
- Constant pain in breasts, they feel very sore when going up or down stairs.
- Breasts seem very full.
- Constant pain in nipples.
- Breasts sensitive to deep pressure.
- Breasts painful; feel as if full of very hard lumps, agg. going up or down stairs.

- Loss of milk while nursing, without known cause.
- 'Galactorrhoea' (many cases).
- Dries up the milk when nursing.
- After two doses of c.m. rapid decrease in size of breasts and quantity of milk in a lady who wanted to wean her child.

18. Clarke J. H. - Dictionary of Practical Materia Medica

Remedies

Pulsatilla pretensis

Symptoms

Female Sexual Organs

- Swelling of breasts, with tensive pain as if the milk rushed into them and caused pressure, while nursing.
- Lumps on breasts of girls before puberty; or escape of thin, milk-like fluid.
- Weeps every time child is put to breast; pain extends into chest, neck, or down back, changes from place to place.
- 'Galactorrhoea' esp. in women who do not nurse their children.
- After weaning, breasts, swell.

19. Clarke J. H. - Dictionary of Practical Materia Medica

Remedies

Ustilago maydis

Clinical

- Agalactia.
- Alopecia.
- Climaxis.
- Dysmenorrhoea.

- Fibroma.
- 'Galactorrhoea'.

20. Gunavante, S. M. - The Genius of Homoeopahic Remedies

Materia Medica
Calcarea carbonica
Female
- 'Galactorrhoea' or deficient milk with breasts flabby; not swollen.

21. Gunavante, S. M. - The Genius of Homoeopahic Remedies

Materia Medica
Phytolacca decandra
Female
- Menses with flow of saliva and tears.
- Swollen or tender mammae.
- Hard nodes in breasts, with enlarged axillary glands.
- 'Galactorrhoea'.
- Cicatrices on mammae inflamed.

22. Herring, C. – Guiding Symptoms of our Materia Medica

Materia Medica
Borax veneta
Pregnancy, Parturition, Lactation
- 'Galactorrhoea'; milk coagulating.
- Milk is too thick and tastes badly; often curdles soon after it has been drawn.
- Milk too copious or too thick.

23. Herring, C. – Guiding Symptoms of our Materia Medica

Materia Medica
Calcarea carbonica

Pregnancy, Parturition, Lactation

- Secretion of milk too abundant; "Galactorrhoea".
- Profuse secretion of watery milk, which the child refuses to take.
- Excessive lactation; also hectic and sweat; debility as a consequence.
- Breasts distended, milk scanty; she is cold, feels cold air very readily; there is a want of vital activity to secrete milk.

24. Herring, C. – Guiding Symptoms of our Materia Medica

Materia Medica

Conium maculatum

Stages of Life, Constitution

- Woman, weak, excitable; "Galactorrhoea".

25. Herring, C. – Guiding Symptoms of our Materia Medica

Materia Medica

Iodium

Pregnancy, parturition, lactation

- Excessive flow of very thin, watery milk; great weakness and rapid emaciation.
- 'Galactorrhoea'.

26. Herring, C. – Guiding Symptoms of our Materia Medica

Materia Medica

Iodium

Stages of Life, Constitution

- Woman, aet. 22, medium height, blue eyes, light auburn hair, sanguine-nervous temperament, predisposed to consumption; "Galactorrhoea".

27. Herring, C. – Guiding Symptoms of our Materia Medica

Materia Medica
Jaborandi
Pregnancy, parturition, lactation
- 'Galactorrhoea'.

28. Herring, C. – Guiding Symptoms of our Materia Medica

Materia Medica
Kalium iodatum
Pregnancy, parturition, lactation
- 'Galactorrhoea'.

29. Herring, C. – Guiding Symptoms of our Materia Medica

Materia Medica
Lac caninum
Pregnancy, parturition, lactation
- Knots and cakes in breast, after miscarriage.
- 'Galactorrhoea'.
- Serviceable in almost all cases where it is required to dry up milk.

30. Herring, C. – Guiding Symptoms of our Materia Medica

Materia Medica
Pulsatilla pretansis
Pregnancy, parturition, lactation
- Milk thin and watery, the true milk globule almost entirely absent.
- Painful sticking and discharge of thin, acrid milk.
- 'Galactorrhoea', particularly in women who are not nursing their children.
- Swelling of breasts.
- After weaning: breasts swell, feel stretched, tense, intensely sore; milk continues to be secreted.

- Mammae: lumps in breasts of girls before puberty; or, escape of thin, milk-white fluid.
- Breast swollen; rheumatic pains extend to muscles of chest, also to shoulders, neck, axillae and down arms, change from place to place; during nursing.
- Swelling of breasts, with pressing tension as if milk would appear in them.

31. Herring, C. – Guiding Symptoms of our Materia Medica

Materia Medica

Rhus toxicodendrone

Pregnancy, parturition, lactation

- Mammae: swell from catching cold, streaks of inflammation; "Galactorrhoea"; milk vanishes with general heat.

32. Herring, C. – Guiding Symptoms of our Materia Medica

Materia Medica

Ustilago maydis

Pregnancy, parturition, lactation

- 'Galactorrhoea'.

33. Hughes, R. and Dake J. P. - A Cyclopedia of Drug Pathogenesy

Conium maculatum

Poisonings

- On their cessation the "Galactorrhoea" returned.
- The lady took 7 grams of extract a day.
- The breasts became emaciated to baggy flaccid skin, and never returned.

34. Hughes, R. – A Manual of Pharmacodynamics

Materia Medica

Iodium

- In such patients prostatitis in the male, and amenorrhoea, "Galactorrhoea" and leucorrhoea in the female subject have been cured by it.

35. Jullian, O. A. – Materia Medica of New Homoeopathic Remedies

Thioproperazinum
Endocrine
- Pituitary disturbance: amenorrhoea, "Galactorrhoea", pseudo-pregnancy.
- Disturbance of the thyroid: hypothyroidism with increase in weight.

36. Jullian, O. A. – Materia Medica of New Homoeopathic Remedies

Thioproperazinum
Symptomatology
Female genital
- 'Galactorrhoea'.
- Amenorrhoea.

37. Jullian, O. A. – Materia Medica of New Homoeopathic Remedies

Thioproperazinum
Symptomatology
Differential Diagnosis
Tuberculinium
- Sensitive to cold, palpitations, "Galactorrhoea", twinges in the shoulders.
- Libido disorders, often stronger or violent, dry skin.

38. Lesser, O. – Text Book of Homoeopathic Materia Medica

The Bor- Aluminium Group iii
Boron
Remedy

Borax veneta
Trophic and Nutritional Disturbances of Nurslings
- To this is added that borax also influences the milk secretion of the mother; the milk is too thick, tastes badly and coagulates rapidly. In lactating young mothers, if the secretion of milk does not cease, the use of borax solution externally gives results. It is in the sense that the clinical indication "''Galactorrhoea''" is meant.

39. Lesser, O. – Text Book of Homoeopathic Materia Medica
The Bor- Aluminium Group iii
Boron
Remedy
Borax veneta
Summary
Leading Symptoms
- Nursing pain in the empty breast of the mother; ''Galactorrhoea''.

40. Lilienthal, S., - Homoeopathic Therapeutics
Homoeopathic Therapeutics
Mammae
Aconitum napellus
- Milk fever with delirium, mammae hot, hard, tense, with scanty milk; ''Galactorrhoea'', but flow nearly stopped by catching cold or emotion, with fear, restlessness, anxiety.

41. Lilienthal, S., - Homoeopathic Therapeutics
Homoeopathic Therapeutics
Nursing and Lactation
Sore and Bleeding Nipples during Nursing
Silicea terra

- Puls. is the best remedy to arrest the secretion of milk after WEANING the child, or to prevent the secondary ailments of weaning., Bell., Bry., Calc. are likewise useful.
- 'Galactorrhoea' requires Calc., especially when the breasts are turgid with milk. Try, moreover: Bell., Bor., Bry., Rhus; or, Chin., Con., Lyc., Phos. ac., Phos., Puls., Stram., Sil., Sulph.

42. Lilienthal, S., - Homoeopathic Therapeutics

Homoeopathic Therapeutics

'Galactorrhoea'

43. Lippe, Adolf Von. – Key Notes and Redline Symptoms of the Materia Medica

Part I

Lac caninum

- Breasts inflamed, painful, aggravated by least jar; must hold them when stepping up or down stairs (Bell.)
- Breasts and throat get sore at every menstrual period
- MASTITIS: BREASTS VERY SORE AND TENDER; CANNOT BEAR A JAR OF THE BED.
- Serviceable in almost all cases when it is required to dry up milk (Asaf.; to bring back or increase it-Lac-D.).
- 'Galactorrhoea' (Asaf., Bry., Puls.).
- Breasts swollen, painful, sensitive before and during menses (Con.).

44. Lippe, Adolf Von. – Key Notes and Redline Symptoms of the Materia Medica

Part II

Phytolacca decandra

- 'Galactorrhoea' (Bell., Bry., Calc., Puls.).

- BREASTS VERY HARD, SWOLLEN, HOT AND PAINFUL (Bell., Merc., Sil.).
- Mammæ full of hard, painful nodosities (Carb-An., Sil.).

45. Lippe, Adolf Von. – Text Book of Materia Medica

Materia Medica
Calcarea carbonicum
- Hot swelling of the mammae.
- Secretion of milk too abundant, ("Galactorrhoea",) or suppressed.

46. Lippe, Adolf Von. – Text Book of Materia Medica

Materia Medica
Rhus toxicodendron
Genital Organs
- 'Galactorrhoea' or suppression of the milk, with burning over the body.

47. Phatak, S. R. – Materia Medica of Homoeopathic Medicines

Materia Medica
Lac caninum
Female
- Breast swollen, painful agg. least jar; has to hold breast firmly when going up and down; before menses; amel. on appearance of menses.
- Constant pain in nipples.
- DRIES UP MILK.
- 'Galactorrhoea'.
- Milk scanty.

48. Phatak, S. R. – Materia Medica of Homoeopathic Medicines

Materia Medica

Phytolacca decandra
Female
- Heavy, Stony, Hard, Swollen or Tender Mammae; paining during suckling; spreading all over the body.
- Hard nodes in breast; with enlarged axillary glands.
- Irritable breast before and during menses.
- 'Galactorrhoea'.
- Bloody, watery discharge from mammae.

49. Phatak, S. R. – Materia Medica of Homoeopathic Medicines

Materia Medica
Pulsatilla pretensis
Female
- Mammae; sore aching; lumps in; in girls before puberty.
- Thin milky fluid escapes from mammae in virgins; before puberty.
- Swelling of breasts after weaning.
- 'Galactorrhoea'.
- Secretion of milk during menses.

50. Vithoulkas, G., - Materia Medica Viva

Borax veneta
Generalities
Genitalia Female
- 'Galactorrhoea'.
- Menses during lactation.

51. Vithoulkas, G., - Materia Medica Viva

Calcarea carbonica
Generalities
Genitalia Female
Lactation disturbances are prominent. Secretion

of milk too abundant; "Galactorrhoea".
Excessive lactation; also hectic and sweat;
weakness as a consequence.

- Mammae painful as if ulcerated, especially to the
touch. Nipples cracked, ulcerated, and very
tender.

52. Yingling, W. A. – Accouncheurs Emergency Manual

Materia Medica

Lac caninum

Generalities

- Breasts sore, sensitive, painful.
- 'Galactorrhoea'.
- Knots and cakes in breasts, after miscarriage.
- Dries up the milk.

<u>Rubrics related with 'Galactorrhoea' in various repertories-</u>

- ## Clarke J. H. - Clinical Repertory-

1. Clinical - B - breast - abscess of
   phos.
2. Clinical - B - breast - affections of
   aur-s. *Cimic.* com. *Con.* hall helon. hep. hyper. iod. lepi. ol-an. onos. orig. paraf. phel. *Phyt.* sulph. zinc.
3. Clinical - B - breast - atrophy of
   chim. onos. sabal
4. Clinical - B - breast - cancer of
   bad. bar-i. brom. carb-an. chim. graph. lob-e. sars. scir.
5. Clinical - B - breast - eruption on
   pip-n.
6. Clinical - B - breast - erysipelas of
   carb-v.
7. Clinical - B - breast - fistula of
   phos.
8. Clinical - B - breast - indurations of
   calc-f. graph.
9. Clinical - B - breast - inflammation of
   acon-l. *Bry.* plan. sabal
10. Clinical - B - breast - nodosities in
    calen.
11. Clinical - B - breast - pain - behind
    Puls.
12. Clinical - B - breast - pain - below
    Ran-b. raph.
13. Clinical - B - breast - pain - between
    raph.

14. Clinical - B - breast - pain - in
iodof. merl. murx. oena. prun. stry. sumb.

15. Clinical - B - breast - painful
Calc. con. lac-c. oci. sabal sol-t-ae. spira.

16. Clinical - B - breast - scirrhus of
sars.

17. Clinical - B - breast - sensitive
syph.

18. Clinical - B - breast - sinuses in
Sil.

19. Clinical - B - breast - sore
symph.

20. Clinical - B - breast - suppuration of
Calen.

21. Clinical - B - breast - swelling of
merl. pip-n. sol-a. sol-o.

22. Clinical - B - breast - tumours of
ars-i. brom. calc-i. chim. cund. ferr-i. hecla
merc-i-f. phase. *Sang.* scroph-xyz. skook. tep.

23. Clinical - B - breast - ulceration of
paeon.

24. Clinical - C - cancer - breast of
graph.

25. Clinical - B - breast - cancer of
bad. bar-i. brom. carb-an. chim. graph. lob-e.
sars. scir.

26. Clinical - M - menstruation - breast painful
during
calc. con. *Sang.*

27. Clinical - B - breast - painful
Calc. con. lac-c. oci. sabal sol-t-ae. spira.

28. Clinical - P - pregnancy - breasts painful
during

Con.

29. Clinical - T - tumours - breast of
     brom. calc-i.

30. Clinical - M - mammae affections of
     aur-s.

• **Choudhury H. – Hints for Treatment of Cancer**

31. Hints for Treatment of Cancer - CANCER OF -
     breast
     alumn. *Apis* ARG-N. arn. ARS. ars-i. *Aster.*
     Aur-ar. aur-m-n. *Bad.* bar-i. bell. bell-p. *Brom.*
     bry. BUFO cadm-i. cadm-s. calc. *Carb-ac. Carb-*
     an. carb-v. carbn-s. *Carc.* caust. cham. *Chin.*
     cist. *Clem.* coloc. CON. CUND. ferr-i. form-ac.
     Gali. GRAPH. hep. *Hydr.* iod. kali-c. kali-i.
     kreos. lac-c. *Lach.* lyc. MERC. merc-i-f. nat-c.
     nit-ac. ol-an. *Ox-ac. Phos. Phyt.* plb-i. *Psor.* puls.
     Sang. Scir. scroph-n. sep. SIL. *Sulph.* thiosin.
     Thuj. tub.

• **Sukumaran N. – Main Symptoms of Heart**
Problems

32. Main Symptoms of Heart Problems -
     STITCHES - breast
     ant-c. caust.

• **Boger C. Boenninghaussen - Boger C.**
Boenninghaussen's Repertory

33. APPETITE - Aversion - milk - of breast
     CINA MERC. nat-c. rheum SIL. *Stann.*

34. NAUSEA AND VOMITING - Aggravation -
     milk - of breast
     sil.

35. COUGH - Excited or aggravated by - motion - of breast

anac. bar-c. CHIN. cocc. dros. LACH. mang. merc. mur-ac. nat-m. NUX-V. PHOS. sil. STANN.

36. CHEST - Aggravation - nursing - the opposite breast

Borx.

- **S. R. Phatak- Concise Repertory**

37. A - Axillae - glands enlarged - breast pain in with

lac-ac.

38. A - Axillae - glands enlarged - hard

aster. carb-an. iod. sil.

39. C - Cough - breast; with coldness of left

nat-c.

40. H - Hot - water as if - breast to abdomen

sang.

41. M - Menses - absent suppressed amenorrhoea - milk in breast with

phos. rhus-t.

42. N - Navel and region - breast to

pall.

43. O - Ovaries - breast - to

lil-t. murx. senec.

44. O - Ovaries - breast - with

sabal

45. T - Teeth - alternating sides - breast with left

kali-c.

46. HEAT AND FEVER IN GENERAL - Partial heat - partial heat - in mammae

47. FACE - Chin - pocks

iod.

48. F - Female organs - upward going - left - mammae to
murx.
49. H - Heart - arms to - left - mammae from
lith-c.
50. L - Leucorrhoea - mammae sore with
dulc.
51. M - Mammae
bell. bry. carb-an. cham. *Con.* hydr. iod. lac-c. merc. oci. phel. *Phos. Phyt.* sabal sil. urt-u.
52. M - Mammae - right
ign. kali-bi. *Phel.* SIL.
53. M - Mammae - right - below
carb-an. caust. chel. CIMIC. *Graph.* laur. lil-t. merc-i-r. *Phos. Sulph.* ust.
54. M - Mammae - right - jumping alive as if
croc.
55. M - Mammae - right - scapula to
merc.
56. M - Mammae - left
borx. bov. *Lil-t. Lyc. Phel.*
57. M - Mammae - left - arms to fingers
aster.
58. M - Mammae - left - below
apis bry. cimic. phos. sulph. thlas. ust.
59. M - Mammae - left - pain - cough with
mosch.
60. M - Mammae - left - pain - drawn back as if
croc.
61. M - Mammae - left - pain - dysmenorrhoea with
caust.
62. M - Mammae - left - pain - head to

glon.

63. M - Mammae - left - pain - jumping
croc.

64. M - Mammae - left - pain - meals after
rumx. stront-c.

65. M - Mammae - left - pain - meals after
rumx. stront-c.

66. M - Mammae - left - pain - menses - between
ust.

67. M - Mammae - left - pain - scapula to
com.

68. M - Mammae - alternating sides - teeth with
kali-c.

69. M - Mammae - abdomen to
phel. sang.

70. M - Mammae - abdomen to - hot water
running from
sang.

71. M - Mammae - abscess
hep. merc. phos. phyt. sil. sulph.

72. M - Mammae - abscess - threatening in old
cicatrices
acet-ac. *Graph. Phyt.*

73. M - Mammae - aching - nursing amel
phel.

74. M - Mammae - arms to
lith-c.

75. M - Mammae - axilla to
brom.

76. M - Mammae - backward
CROT-T. laur. lil-t. til.

77. M - Mammae - backward - left
form.

78.   M - Mammae - backward - drawn
croc.

79.   M - Mammae - ball below
hura

80.   M - Mammae - bares
camph.

81.   M - Mammae - burning
cimic. laur. sulph.

82.   M - Mammae - burning - below - right
aeth. phos.

83.   M - Mammae - burning - below - left
laur. mur-ac. rumx.

84.   M - Mammae - burning - motion amel
ars.

85.   M - Mammae - caking milk of
nux-v.

86.   M - Mammae - cancer
aster. aur-m. bad. brom. bufo con. cund.
graph. hydr. merc. phos. sil.

87.   M - Mammae - cancer - itching with
sil.

88.   M - Mammae - cancer - stitches in shoulders
and uterus with
clem.

89.   M - Mammae - cancer - swelling of axillary
glands with
goss.

90.   M - Mammae - chilliness in
cocc. guaj.

91.   M - Mammae - cicatrices - old
carb-an. *Graph. Phyt.*

92.   M - Mammae - cicatrices - suppurating
sil.

93.   M - Mammae - cold
cocc. med.

94.   M - Mammae - cold - agg
sabal

95.   M - Mammae - cold - left
nat-c.

96.   M - Mammae - cold - left - coughing while
nat-c.

97.   M - Mammae - congested
acon. apis ferr. phos.

98.   M - Mammae - congested - milk with insanity
in
bell. stram.

99.   M - Mammae - coughing agg
con.

100.   M - Mammae - cramp
plat.

101.   M - Mammae - crawling - left
ant-t.

102.   M - Mammae - crawling - cold
guaj.

103.   M - Mammae - dwindled emaciated
ars-i. bar-c. cham. chin. *Coff.* CON. ferr. IOD.
Kali-i. nat-m. nit-ac. *Nux-m.* sabal sec. sil.

104.   M - Mammae - dwindled emaciated - lump
hard small painful with
kreos.

105.   M - Mammae - dwindled emaciated - ovaries
with
bar-c.

106.   M - Mammae - emptiness after child nurses
borx.

107.   M - Mammae - enlarged as if

calc-p. cycl. sep.

108. M - Mammae - eruption
caust. psor.

109. M - Mammae - eruption - herpes nursing
women in
dulc.

110. M - Mammae - erysipelas
apis

111. M - Mammae - everything affects
phyt.

112. M - Mammae - fingers to
aster. lith-c.

113. M - Mammae - fistula
phos. sil.

114. M - Mammae - flaccid
con. iod.

115. M - Mammae - flowing milk as if in
dict. kreos. nux-v. puls.

116. M - Mammae - hard indurated
aster. bry. *Carb-an.* cham. con. graph. phyt.
plb. *Sil.*

117. M - Mammae - hard indurated - menses
absent with
dulc.

118. M - Mammae - hard indurated - nodes
aster. nit-ac.

119. M - Mammae - hard indurated - small and
colic during
plb.

120. M - Mammae - head to
lac-ac.

121. M - Mammae - heavy
bry. chin. iod. lac-c. phyt.

122. M - Mammae - hypertrophy
Calc. chim. *Con. Phyt.*

123. M - Mammae - hypertrophy - climaxis at
sang.

124. M - Mammae - inflamed
bell. bry. hep. phyt. sil. sulph.

125. M - Mammae - inner side arms to fingers
aster.

126. M - Mammae - itching
alum. caust. con.

127. M - Mammae - itching - warm getting on
aeth.

128. M - Mammae - jerks
croc.

129. M - Mammae - large
chim.

130. M - Mammae - menses - before agg
bry. calc. *Con.* KALI-M. LAC-C. lyc. ol-an.
Phyt. puls.

131. M - Mammae - menses - during agg
con. helon. lac-c. merc. murx. phel. phos. phyt.
zinc.

132. M - Mammae - milk present - absent menses
with
bell. bry. calc. lyc. phos. puls. rhus-t. sabin.
stram.

133. M - Mammae - milk present - boys in
merc.

134. M - Mammae - milk present - increased
acon.

135. M - Mammae - milk present - insanity during
bell. stram.

136. M - Mammae - milk present - menses - during

calc. merc. pall. puls. tub.

137. M - Mammae - milk present - menses - instead of

merc.

138. M - Mammae - milk present - painless gathering from not nursing

nux-v.

139. M - Mammae - milk present - virgins non-pregnant women in

asaf. cycl. lyc. *Merc.* PULS. thlas. tub. urt-u.

140. M - Mammae - neuralgia left

sumb.

141. M - Mammae - night agg

bufo

142. M - Mammae - nodes in

bell-p. calc-f. *Carb-an. Con.* crot-t. lyc. *Phyt.* SIL. tub.

143. M - Mammae - nodes in - black points on skin with

iod.

144. M - Mammae - nodes in - girls puberty before

puls.

145. M - Mammae - nodes in - hard burning

lyc.

146. M - Mammae - nodes in - knots in axilla with

merc-i-f.

147. M - Mammae - nodes in - milk secretion of with

chim.

148. M - Mammae - nodes in - movable tender moving arms agg

calc-i.

149. M - Mammae - nodes in - old

150. M - Mammae - nodes in - painful old fat men in
bar-c.

151. M - Mammae - nodes in - skin on
iod.

152. M - Mammae - nodes in - soft tender
kali-m. puls.

153. M - Mammae - nodes in - touch agg
ars-i.

154. M - Mammae - nodes in - walnut like males in
bar-c. calc-p.

155. M - Mammae - numb
graph.

156. M - Mammae - nursing agg
phel.

157. M - Mammae - outward dartings
arg-met. clem. ol-an.

158. M - Mammae - outward dartings - menses during
grat.

159. M - Mammae - presses hard hand with
cimic. con.

160. M - Mammae - radiating from
phyt.

161. M - Mammae - rivet or bullet feeling of in region
lil-t.

162. M - Mammae - shivering over
cocc. guaj.

163. M - Mammae - shooting
polyg-h.

164. M - Mammae - shoulder to - between

phel.

165. M - Mammae - shoulder to - left
sang.

166. M - Mammae - shuddering in with goose flesh
guaj.

167. M - Mammae - small undeveloped
iod. lyc. nux-m. onos. sabal sulph.

168. M - Mammae - small undeveloped - one than other
sabal

169. M - Mammae - sore painful
arn. bell. bry. calc. cham. *Con.* helon. kali-m. LAC-C. lyc. med. merc. onos. phyt. puls. sabal sil. syph.

170. M - Mammae - sore painful - axillary glands enlargement with
ac-ac.

171. M - Mammae - sore painful - bath cold agg
sabal

172. M - Mammae - sore painful - climaxis at
sang.

173. M - Mammae - sore painful - dysmenorrhoea with
canth. sars.

174. M - Mammae - sore painful - infants
cham.

175. M - Mammae - sore painful - menses - at the beginning of
tub.

176. M - Mammae - sore painful - menses - absent with
dulc. zinc.

177. M - Mammae - sore painful - menses - during

or other time
grat. med. murx. syph.

178. M - Mammae - sore painful - pregnancy during
calc-p.

179. M - Mammae - sore painful - rubbing hard amel
rad-br.

180. M - Mammae - sore painful - ezing agg
hydr.

181. M - Mammae - sore painful - stooping when
grat.

182. M - Mammae - sore painful - urination agg
clem.

183. M - Mammae - sore painful - yawning agg
mag-c.

184. M - Mammae - stitches
apis carb-an. *Con. Nit-ac.* sil.

185. M - Mammae - stitches - dysmenorrhoea with
caust.

186. M - Mammae - stitches - nursing when
calc.

187. M - Mammae - suckling while - agg
ant-t. borx. bry. crot-t. lac-c. lil-t. phel. phyt. *Puls.* sil.

188. M - Mammae - suckling while - amel
phel.

189. M - Mammae - suckling while - cramps
cham.

190. M - Mammae - suckling while - pain in opposite
borx.

191. M - Mammae - swelled

Bell. BRY. con. helon. hep. *Phos.* PHYT. PULS. *Sil.* sulph. urt-u.

192. M - Mammae - swelled - as if
    calc-p.

193. M - Mammae - swelled - bath cold agg
    sabal

194. M - Mammae - swelled - climaxis at
    sang.

195. M - Mammae - swelled - inguinal glands with
    oci.

196. M - Mammae - swelled - lancinating pain
    aeth.

197. M - Mammae - swelled - leucorrhoea with
    dulc.

198. M - Mammae - swelled - menses - after
    secretion of milk with
    cycl.

199. M - Mammae - swelled - menses - instead of
    dulc. rat.

200. M - Mammae - swelled - milk secretion of with
    asaf. cycl. tub.

201. M - Mammae - swelled - weaning after
    all-s. puls.

202. M - Mammae - throbbing
    borx.

203. M - Mammae - tingling
    sabin.

204. M - Mammae - ulceration
    hep. phyt. sil.

205. M - Mammae - uterus with
    sil.

206. M - Mammae - warts
    castor-eq.

207. M - Menses - absent suppressed amenorrhoea
- mammae scirrhus of with
brom.

208. M - Menses - absent suppressed amenorrhoea
- milk in breast with
phos. rhus-t.

209. M - Menses - absent suppressed amenorrhoea
- weaning after
sep.

210. M - Menses - absent suppressed amenorrhoea
- wet getting feet from
puls. rhus-t.

211. M - Menses - delayed in girls at puberty -
mammae undeveloped with
lyc.

212. M - Menses - delayed in girls at puberty - milk
drinking much from
lac-d.

213. M - Menses - mammae agg
bry. calc. lac-c.

214. M - Mumps - metastasis - mammae to
Puls.

- **Herbert A. Roberts - Sensation As If**
215. Mouth tongue taste teeth gums - Breast were
coming up into her mouth
heed.

216. Female sexual organs - Arrows were forced
through breasts
calc.

217. Female sexual organs - Bullet or rivet in region
of breast
lil-t.

218. Female sexual organs - Burning - in breast a

fire were

castm.

219. Female sexual organs - Crushed breast were being

spig.

220. Female sexual organs - Drawn - through breasts with oppression something painful were

eupi.

221. Female sexual organs - Drop - off breasts would

castor-eq. iod.

222. Female sexual organs - Empty feeling in breasts after being emptied

borx.

223. Female sexual organs - Fall - off breasts would

castor-eq. hall iod.

224. Female sexual organs - Fire - were burning in breast

castm.

225. Female sexual organs - Forced - through breasts arrows were

calc.

226. Female sexual organs - Full - within and below breasts were

fl-ac.

227. Female sexual organs - Full - of hard lumps breasts were

lac-c.

228. Female sexual organs - Bruised - in left breast

arum-t.

229. Female sexual organs - Fuller than usual breasts were

230. Female sexual organs - Heaviness in breasts

231. Female sexual organs - Hot water were pouring from breast into abdomen

232. Female sexual organs - Ice balls of ice dropped from each breast through to back and rolling down back along legs and off

233. Female sexual organs - Insects were crawling over left breast

234. Female sexual organs - Irons torn with red hot in left breast

235. Female sexual organs - Knives - were thrust into breast

236. Female sexual organs - Larger breast were

237. Female sexual organs - Lumps breasts were full of hard

238. Female sexual organs - Milk - would appear in breast

239. Female sexual organs - Milk - were coming into right breast

240. Female sexual organs - Milk - reached into breasts

241. Female sexual organs - Needles - sticking in left breast
con.

242. Female sexual organs - Rivet or bullet in region of breasts
lil-t.

243. Female sexual organs - Rose higher hard induration in breast
carb-an.

244. Female sexual organs - Sticking - in left breast needles were
con.

245. Female sexual organs - String - were pulling in right breast
sumb.

246. Female sexual organs - String - were pulling from breast into axilla
brom.

247. Female sexual organs - Suppurate - breast would
calc. clem.

248. Female sexual organs - Suppurate - breast would if touched
calc.

249. Female sexual organs - Swollen - breasts were
berb.

250. Female sexual organs - Thrust - into breast knives were
hydr.

251. Female sexual organs - Torn - toward abdomen breast were
bufo

252. Female sexual organs - Torn - toward body

breasts were

bufo

253. Female sexual organs - Torn - with red-hot irons in left breasts

chinin-ar.

254. Female sexual organs - Torn - to pieces heart and breasts were

hyos.

255. Female sexual organs - Ulcer - a deep had formed in left breast

iodof.

256. Female sexual organs - Ulcerated - breasts would

merc.

257. Female sexual organs - Water - hot were pouring from breast into abdomen

sang.

258. Internal chest - Anxiety below left breast

phos.

259. Internal chest - Crowbar were pressed tightly from right to left breast until it came and twisted a knot around the

tab.

260. Internal chest - Drawn - back in left breast by means of a thread something were

croc.

261. Internal chest - Hand grasped her breast bone

sil.

262. Internal chest - Pressed - tightly from right to left breast a crowbar were

263. Internal chest - String - left breast were drawn toward back by a

croc.

264. External chest - Induration hard rose higher in breast
carb-an.

265. Heart and circulation - Crowbar were pressed tightly from right to left breast - twisted a knot around heart which stopped it and
tab.

266. Heart and circulation - Stopped - by a crowbar which pressed tightly from right to left breast and twisted a knot around heart
tab.

267. Heart and circulation - Torn - to pieces heart and breast were
hyos.

268. Neck and back - Balls hot dropped from each breast through to back - rolling down back along each limb and dropping off at heels followed by balls of ice
lyc.

269. Lower extremities - Balls - hot dropped from each breast through to back and rolling down back along each limb and off
lyc.

270. Female sexual organs - Abscesses in mammae
crot-c. sil.

271. Female sexual organs - Bladder were pressing outward in mammae
lact.

272. Female sexual organs - Cord around right mamma
lepi.

273. Female sexual organs - Crawling - insects above the left mamma

ant-t.

274. Female sexual organs - Enlarged - mammary glands were

sep.

275. Female sexual organs - Flea-bites - on left mamma

am-m.

276. Female sexual organs - Pressing - outward in mamma bladder were

lact.

277. Female sexual organs - Pulled inward left mamma were

aster.

278. Female sexual organs - Swelling - mammae were

benz-ac. berb.

279. Female sexual organs - Swelling - mammae were

benz-ac. berb.

280. Female sexual organs - Tongs left mammary region were torn with red-hot

chinin-ar.

281. Female sexual organs - Touched mammary glands would suppurate if

calc. clem.

282. External chest - Biting between mammae fleas were

ph-ac.

283. External chest - Fleas - biting between mammae

ph-ac.

- **Boericke, Oscar - Repertory**

284. FEMALE SEXUAL SYSTEM - Lactation - Milk
- Too profuse - galactorrhea
bell. *Borx. Calc.* cham. chim. *Con.* erig. iod. lac-
c. lact. *Medus.* parth. phos. phyt. pip-m. rheum
ric. sabal *Salv.* sec. *Sol-o.* spira. ust.

285. FEMALE SEXUAL SYSTEM - Mammae - Pain
in breasts
acon. all-s. apis arg-n. *Aster.* aur-s. *Bell.* brom.
Bry. Calc. carb-an. cham. *Chim. Cimic. Con.* cot.
croc. *Crot-t. Hep.* hydr. hyper. *Lac-ac.* lac-c.
lach. *Lap-a.* lepi. med. *Merc.* merl. *Murx.* nat-m.
onos. pall. *Phel. Phos. Phyt.* plb. *Plb-i.* polyg-h.
prun. psor. puls. *Sang.* sil. sumb. zinc.

286. FEMALE SEXUAL SYSTEM - Mammae - Pain
in breasts - Inframammary
Cimic. puls. *Ran-b.* raph. sumb. ust. zinc.

287. FEMALE SEXUAL SYSTEM - Mammae - Pain
in breasts - Relieved by supporting heavy
mammae
Bry. Lac-c. phyt.

288. FEMALE SEXUAL SYSTEM - Mammae - Pain
in breasts - Worse from jar toward evening
lac-c.

289. FEMALE SEXUAL SYSTEM - Menopause
climacteric period; change of life - Breasts
enlarged painful
sang.

290. FEMALE SEXUAL SYSTEM - Complaints
preceding and attending flow - Breasts - Icy
cold
med.

291. FEMALE SEXUAL SYSTEM - Complaints
preceding and attending flow - Breasts - Milk

in them in place of menses

merc.

292. FEMALE SEXUAL SYSTEM - Complaints
preceding and attending flow - Breasts -
Tender swollen

bry. calc. canth. *Con.* graph. *Helon.* kali-c. *Lac-c.*
mag-c. merc. *Murx. Phyt. Puls.* sang.

293. FEMALE SEXUAL SYSTEM - Abortion - With
- pains - flying across abdomen doubling her
up; chills; pricking in breasts; pains in loins

cimic.

294. FEMALE SEXUAL SYSTEM - Complaints
during pregnancy - Breasts painful -
Inflammatory

Bell. Bry.

295. FEMALE SEXUAL SYSTEM - Complaints
during pregnancy - Breasts painful - Neuralgic

Con. puls.

296. FEMALE SEXUAL SYSTEM - Lactation - Pain
- In opposite breast

borx.

297. RESPIRATORY SYSTEM - Cough -
Concomitant - Left breast feels cold

nat-c.

298. SKIN - Verruca - Situated on - breast

castor-eq.

299. FEVER - Chill - location - Breast

chin.

300. GENERALITIES - Cancer - Of - breast

ars-i. bar-i. brom. bufo *Carb-an.* carc. *Con.*
cund. form-ac. graph. *Hydr.* nat-cac. phyt. *Plb-
i.* scir.

301. GENERALITIES - Injuries - Bruises - Of -

breast

bell-p. *Con.*

302. FEMALE SEXUAL SYSTEM - Mammae - Abscess

bry. crot-t. graph. *Hep. Phos.* phyt. *Sil.* sulph.

303. FEMALE SEXUAL SYSTEM - Mammae - Atrophy

chim. *Con. Iod.* kali-i. nit-ac. onos. *Sabal*

304. FEMALE SEXUAL SYSTEM - Mammae - Cancer - bleeding

kreos. lach. *Phos.* sang. strych-g. thuj.

305. FEMALE SEXUAL SYSTEM - Mammae - Cancer - scirrhous

ars. carb-an. *Con.* cund. hydr. kreos. lap-a. phyt. *Scir. Sil.*

306. FEMALE SEXUAL SYSTEM - Mammae - Induration hardness

alumn. anan. *Aster.* bar-i. bell. *Bry.* bufo *Calc-f. Carb-an.* carb-v. cham. cist. clem. *Con. Graph. Iod.* kreos. lac-c. *Lap-a.* merc. nit-ac. *Phyt. Plb. Plb-i.*

307. FEMALE SEXUAL SYSTEM - Mammae - Inflammation

Acon. ant-t. apis arn. ars. *Bell. Bry.* calc. *Cham.* cist. *Con. Crot-t.* ferr-p. galeg. graph. *Hep. Lac-c.* lach. *Merc. Phel. Phos. Phyt.* plan. *Puls.* sabad. *Sil.* sulph.

308. FEMALE SEXUAL SYSTEM - Mammae - Pain in breasts - Relieved by supporting heavy mammae

Bry. Lac-c. phyt.

309. FEMALE SEXUAL SYSTEM - Mammae - Pain in breasts - Worse from jar toward evening

lac-c.

310. FEMALE SEXUAL SYSTEM - Complaints following menses - Mammae swollen milky secretion
cycl.

311. FEMALE SEXUAL SYSTEM - Parturition labor - Pains - Shifting - Across abdomen doubling her up; pricking in mammae; shivers during first stage
cimic.

312. FEMALE SEXUAL SYSTEM - Uterus - Pain - Neuralgic - right side upward across body thence to left mamma
murx.

313. SKIN - Erysipelas - Mammae
carb-v. sulph.

314. GENERALITIES - Glands - Parotid inflammation parotitis - metastases to - mammae ovaries
con. jab. puls.

315. MAMMAE - General; in
bell. bry. carb-an. cham. *Con.* hydr. iod. lac-c. *Phos. Phyt.* sil.

316. MAMMAE - Right
kali-bi. *Sil.*

317. MAMMAE - Right
kali-bi. *Sil.*

318. MAMMAE - Alternating sides
puls.

319. MAMMAE - Backward
CROT-T. form. laur. lil-t. til.

320. MAMMAE - Backward - left
form.

321. MAMMAE - Backward - left
form.

322. MAMMAE - Lactation
bell. cham. merc. *Puls.* sep. sil.

323. MAMMAE - Menses; agg. before
bry. calc. *Con.* KALI-M. LAC-C. *Phyt.* puls.

324. MAMMAE - Sore painful
arn. calc. con. *Lac-c.* phyt.

325. MAMMAE - Swelled
bell. *Bry.* con. phos. *Phyt. Puls.* sil.

- **Schroyens, Frederick - Synthesis 9.2.1b**

326. MIND - DELUSIONS - nursing; she is - animals or hairy babies
choc.

327. MIND - DELUSIONS - nursing; she is - child; her
atro. thiam.

328. MIND - NAKED wants to be - bares her breast in puerperal mania
Camph.

329. MIND - SHAMELESS - exposing - breasts; the
bung-fa.

330. BACK - PAIN - Dorsal region - Scapulae - right - extending to -Breast near nipple
ang.

331. BACK - PAIN - Dorsal region - Scapulae - right - extending to - Breast near nipple - cutting pain
ang.

332. CHEST - CHICKEN BREAST
kali-c. lac-ac.

333. DREAMS - ABUSING - pinched her breast;

the lady who

bung-fa.

334. DREAMS - BACK - pinched back and breast are

phos.

335. DREAMS - BREAST FED - guru; by one's

phasco-ci.

336. DREAMS - CHILDREN; about - newborns - feeding from dismembered breast

positr.

337. DREAMS - DEATH - dying - man suckling at her breast; dying

sal-.

338. DREAMS - EXPOSING - breast; her

bung-fa.

339. DREAMS - EXPOSING - breast; her - left

bung-fa.

340. DREAMS - EXPOSING - friend is exposing her breast

bung-fa.

341. DREAMS - MEN - breast; men's

phasco-ci.

342. DREAMS - MILK - pressing out milk of her right breast

positr.

343. DREAMS - BACK - pinched back and breast are

phos.

344. DREAMS - SEDUCING - exposing thighs and breasts; by

bung-fa.

345. FEVER - NURSING; from - rheumatic pain in breast

BRY.

346. MIND - DELUSIONS - mammae are too big or too small
bar-c.

347. MIND - FEAR - cancer; of - Mammae
aster.

348. MIND - FEAR - mammae; lumps in
bamb-a.

349. FACE - INFLAMMATION - Parotid glands - metastasis to - Mammae
abrot. carb-v. con. jab. PULS.

350. STOMACH - PAIN - extending to - Mammae
lach. puls.

351. STOMACH - PAIN - extending to - Mammae; near
lach.

352. ABDOMEN - COMPLAINTS of abdomen - extending to - Mammae
plb.

353. ABDOMEN - PAIN - Inguinal region - right - extending to - Mamma; left
MURX.

354. ABDOMEN - PAIN - Inguinal region - extending to - Mamma; left
MURX.

355. ABDOMEN - PAIN - Sides - Flanks - extending to - Mamma; left
alum.

356. ABDOMEN - PAIN - Umbilicus - extending to - Mammae
Pall.

357. ABDOMEN - PAIN - extending to - Mamma; right

358. ABDOMEN - UMBILICUS; complaints of - Region of - extending to - Mammae
pall.

359. BLADDER - PAIN - extending to - Mammae
murx.

360. FEMALE GENITALIA/SEX - MENSES - absent - milk in mammae with
phos. *Rhus-t.*

361. FEMALE GENITALIA/SEX - MENSES - delayed in girls first menses - mammae with undeveloped
lyc.

362. FEMALE GENITALIA/SEX - OVARIES; complaints of - accompanied by - Mammae; complaints of
Sabal

363. FEMALE GENITALIA/SEX - OVARIES; complaints of - extending to - Mammae
lil-t. murx. senec.

364. FEMALE GENITALIA/SEX - PAIN - extending to - Mammae
lach.

365. FEMALE GENITALIA/SEX - PAIN - Ovaries - extending to - Mamma to opposite
murx.

366. FEMALE GENITALIA/SEX - PAIN - Ovaries - extending to - Mammae
senec.

367. FEMALE GENITALIA/SEX - PAIN - Uterus - extending to - Mammae
lyss. murx.

368. FEMALE GENITALIA/SEX - UTERUS;

complaints of - accompanied by - Mammae; complaints of

sil.

369. **CHEST - NIGHT - Mammae**
Bufo

370. **CHEST - ABSCESS - Mammae**
Apis *Arn. Ars. Bell. Bry.* bufo *Camph.* carb-an. cham.. *Cist.* con. *Crot-h.* crot-t. graph. HEP.. kali-chl. kali-i. kreos. *Lach.* MERC.. paeon. PHOS.. PHYT. pyrog. sars. SIL.. SULPH. tarent-c.

371. **CHEST - ATROPHY - Mammae**
anac. anan. ars. bar-c. cham. *Chim.* chin. COFF. CON. dulc. fago. ferr. IOD.. KALI-I. *Kreos.* lac-d. lach. *Nat-m. Nit-ac.. Nux-m.* onos. plb. Sabal sacch. sars. *Sec. Sep.* sil. STAPH. .

372. **CHEST - AXILLA; complaints of - extending to - Mammae**
caust.

373. **CHEST - BALL; sensation of a - Mamma; under left**
hura

374. **CHEST - CANCER - Mammae**
acon. aids. alum. alumn. *Apis* . *Arg-n.* arn.. *Ars.. Ars-i.* ars-s-f. *Aster. Aur-ar.* aur-m. aur-m-n. *Bad.* bapt. bar-i. *Bell.. Bell-p. Brom.* bry. BUFO cadm-met. calc.. calc-i. calc-sil. *Carb-ac. Carb-an..* carb-v.. carbn-s. carc. caust.. cham. *Chim.* cic. cist. *Clem..* coloc. CON.. congo-r. *Cund.* cupr.. cypr. ferr.. ferr-i. form-ac. formal. gaert. *Gali.* GRAPH. *Hep..* hip-ac. hippoz. *Hydr.* ign. iod. kali-br. kali-c.. *Kali-i.* kreos.. lac-c. *Lach..* lap-a. lob-e. *Lyc..* mag-c. MERC.. *Merc-d. Merc-*

i-f. naja nat-cac. nat-tmcy. *Nit-ac.* ol-an. *Ox-ac.* ph-ac. *Phos. Phyt. Plb-i. Psor. Puls.* rad-br. rhus-t. *Sang.* sars. scir. scroph-n. sed-r. semp. *Sep.* SIL. strych-g. sul-i. *Sulph.* tarent. thuj. tub. zinc.

375. **CHEST - CANCER - Mammae - accompanied by - induration of the mammae**
alum-sil. aur-n-f. cadm-calc-f. carc. CON.

376. **CHEST - CANCER - Mammae - accompanied by - swelling of mammae**
cadm-calc-f.

377. **CHEST - CANCER - Mammae - last stage - mastectomy of opposite cancerous mamma; after**
lac-c.

378. **CHEST - CHILLINESS in - Mammae shivering in**
cimic. *Cocc.* con. dig. *Guaj.* nux-v. petr. rhus-t.

379. **CHEST - CICATRICES; old - Mammae; in**
carb-an. GRAPH. *Phyt.*

380. **CHEST - COLD - agg. - Mammae**
Sabal

381. **CHEST - COLDNESS - Mammae**
Bry. chin. cimic. *Cocc.* dig. *Med.* rhus-t.

382. **CHEST - CONGESTION - Mammae**
acon. apis ferr. phos. yohim.

383. **CHEST - CONSTRICTION - Mammae**
lil-t. sang. stram. verat.

384. **CHEST - CONTUSIONS - Mammae**
arn.

385. **CHEST - COUGH - during - agg. - Mammae**
con.

386. CHEST - CRACKS - Mammae
Caust. graph. *Sulph.*

387. CHEST - DISCOLORATION - spots - brown - Mammae; on
cadm-s. carb-v. lyc. phos. *Sep.*

388. CHEST - DISCOLORATION - Mammae - blue - ulcerated mammae; of
bell-p. *Lach.* phos.

389. CHEST - DISTENSION - Mammae
aster. zinc.

390. CHEST - EMACIATION - Mammae
ars-i. bar-c. cench. cham. chin. COFF. *Con.* ferr. iod. *Kali-i.* kreos. lac-d. nat-m. nit-ac. *Nux-m.* *Onos.* sabal sec. sep. sil.

391. CHEST - EMPTINESS sensation of - Mammae
BORX.

392. CHEST - ENLARGED sensation - Mammae
cycl.

393. CHEST - ERUPTIONS - Mammae
amp. arge-pl. ars. aster. bufo *Caust.* falco-pe. graph. grat. hep. led. lyc. nat-m. phos. pip-n. psor. rhus-t. sinus. staph. tab. valer.

394. CHEST - ERUPTIONS - Mammae - furfuraceous between mammae
aster.

395. CHEST - ERYSIPELAS of mammae
acon. anan. APIS$_k$ arn. *Bell. Bry.* cadm-s. *Carb-an. Carb-v. Carbn-s. Cham.* coll. graph. *Phos.* plan. *Sulph.*

396. CHEST - FISTULOUS openings - Mammae; in
alum. *Caust. Hep. Merc. Phos. Phyt.* SIL.

397. CHEST - FLABBY mammae
bell. calc. cham. CON. graph. hydr. IOD.

kali-i. kreos. nit-ac., nux-m., nux-v. onos.st
sars.,

398. **CHEST - FLUTTERING - Mammae**
plut-n.

399. **CHEST - FORMICATION - Mammae**
calc. chin., con., mang. ran-s. sabin.,

400. **CHEST - FULLNESS - Mammae**
bell. *Bry.,* calc. *Calc-p.* choc. clem. cycl. *Dulc.*
Kali-c. Lac-c. lact. merc. nux-v. phos. *Phyt.* plut-
n. sabal sec. *Sep.* spect. zinc.

401. **CHEST - FULLNESS - Mammae - sensation of**
fullness - milk in mammae; as if
choc.

402. **CHEST - GURGLING - Mammae**
crot-t.

403. **CHEST - HEAT - Mammae**
Acon. Apis arn. ARS. bar-c. bell. benz-ac. bry.
calc., calc-p. *Cann-s., Carb-an.* carb-v. cham.
clem. cocc. con. graph. hep. laur. lyc. *Merc.* nit-
ac. phos. phyt. *Puls.* rhus-t. sep. *Sil.* SULPH.

404. **CHEST - HYPERTROPHY - Mammae**
bell., bell-p. bry., *Calc.* calc-p. chim. *Con.* cycl.
hep., hydrog. iod. kali-i. med. nat-m., *Nux-v.,*
petr-ra. phos., *Phyt.* sep. sulph.,

405. **CHEST - INDURATION - Mammae**
alum-sil. alumn. ambr., anan. apis ars., *Ars-i.*
Aster. Aur. BAR-I. *Bell., Bry.,* bufo *Calc.,* calc-f.
calc-i. calc-p. CARB-AN., *Carb-v. Carbn-s.*
CHAM., chim. *Cist. Clem..,* coloc. CON., *Crot-h.*
Crot-t. cund. *Cupr.* cycl. dulc. *Graph.,* hep.
Hydr. hyos. ina-i., *Iod.,* KALI-CHL. *Kali-m.*
Kreos. Lac-c. lap-a. *Lyc.* mang., *Merc.,* nit-ac.,
petr., *Phos., Phyt.* plb., *Plb-i.* puls., *Rhus-t.,* rutak

   Dr. Rajneesh Kumar Sharma

sabin. *Sep.* SIL. spong. sul-i. *Sulph. Thuj.* tub. ust. vip.

406. **CHEST - INFLAMMATION - Mammae**
Acon. acon-l. anan. ant-t. *Apis* arn. ars. BELL. bell-p. BRY. bufo *Cact.* calc. CAMPH. *Carb-an. Carb-v. Carbn-s.* carc. *Card-m. Castor-eq. Cham. Cist.* clem. *Con. Crot-t.* cur. dulc. ferr. ferr-p. galeg. graph. HEP. lac-ac. lac-c. *Lach.* laur. *Lyc. Merc. Merc-d.* naphthoq. op. petr. phel. *Phos.* PHYT. plan. plb. *Puls.* pyrog. rhus-t. sabad. sabal *Samb.* SIL. SULPH. ust. verat-v. x-ray

407. **CHEST - INJURIES - Mammae; to**
arn. ars-i. *Bell-p.* calen. carb-an. con. *Cund.* kali-chl. phos. ruta

408. **CHEST - INTERTRIGO - Mammae**
syc.

409. **CHEST - ITCHING - Mammae**
agar. alum. alum-p. anac. ang. ant-c. arge-pl. arn. ars. bar-c. bar-s. berb. bov. calc. canth. carb-v. carbn-s. castor-eq. *Caust.* CON. *Dulc.* hipp. jug-r. *Kali-c.* led. lyc. mez. nat-m. nicc. nux-v. phel. *Phos.* plb. ran-s. rhus-t. ribo. sabad. sep. sil. spong. squil. staph. sulph.

410. **CHEST - JERKS - Mammae**
croc.

411. **CHEST - LARGE - Mammae**
chim.

412. **CHEST - LUMPS - Mammae; between**
raph.

413. **CHEST - MAMMAE; complaints of**
acon. alum. am-c. ambr. *Apis Arn. Ars.* asaf. bar-c. *Bell.* borx. BRY. bufo *Calc.* camph.

cann-s. CARB-AN. carb-v. caust. CHAM.
chim. *Clem.* cocc. coloc. CON. croc. cupr.
dig. dulc. ferr. graph. guaj. *Hep.* hydr. iod.
kali-c. kreos. lac-ac. lac-c. laur. lepi. lyc.
mang. merc. mez. nat-c. nat-m. nit-ac. nux-
m. nux-v. oci. op. orig. petr. ph-ac. phel.
PHOS. PHYT. plb. *Puls.* ran-s. rheum rhus-t.
ruta sabal sabin. samb. scroph-n. sep. SIL.
Sulph. thuj. urt-u. verat. zinc.

414. **CHEST - MENSES - after - agg. - Mammae**
berb. cycl.

415. **CHEST - MENSES - before - agg. - Mammae**
bry. calc. *Con.* KALI-M. LAC-C. lyc. ol-an.
Phyt. puls.

416. **CHEST - MENSES - during - agg. - Mammae**
berb. bry. *Calc.* carb-an. *Caust. Cham.* CON.
dulc. grat. *Helo.* helon. *Iod. Lac-c.* merc. murx.
phel. PHOS. PHYT. rhus-t. sang. thuj. vib.
zinc.

417. **CHEST - NODULES sensitive - Mammae**
aids. arn. ARS. aur. *Bell. Bell-p. Bry. Bufo* calc-
f. calc-i. calc-p. CARB-AN. *Carb-v.* cham.
Chim. chin. cist. clem. *Coloc.* CON. croc. crot-
t. cund. cupr. dulc. *Graph. Iod.* kali-c. kreos.
Lac-c. lac-h. *Lyc.* mang. merc. *Merc-d.* nat-m.
Nit-ac. Phos. PHYT. *Puls.* rhus-t. ruta sang.
scir. scroph-n. sep. SIL. *Sulph.* thuj. tub. vanil.

418. **CHEST - NUMBNESS - Mammae**
graph.

419. **CHEST - NURSING - agg. - Mammae**
ant-t. borx. bry. crot-t. lac-c. lil-t. phel. phyt.
Puls. sil.

420. **CHEST - NURSING - agg. - Mammae -**

Opposite mamma

borx.

421.   **CHEST - NURSING - amel. - Mammae**
phel.

422.   **CHEST - OPPRESSION - Mammae**
allox. bry. calc. chin. clem. hyos. *Iod.* lac-c. lil-t.
petr-ra. phyt. plut-n. tax. thuj. tritic-vg..

423.   **CHEST - PAIN - Axillae - extending to -
Mammae**
caust.

424.   **CHEST - PAIN - Mammae**
acon. aesc. aeth. agath-a. aids. all-s. allox. aln.
aloe alum. *Am-c.* am-m. ambr. anan. ant-c. apis
arg-n. arn.. *Ars.* ars-i. arum-t. *Asc-t.* aster. aur.
aur-s. bamb-a.. bar-c. bar-i. BELL. berb. *Borx.*
Bov. brom. *Bry. Bufo*k cact. calad. *Calc.* calc-i.
calc-p. calc-sil. *Cann-s..* canth. *Carb-an..* carb-v.
carbn-s. cartl-s. *Cham.. Chim.* chinin-ar. chinin-
s. chir-fl. cic. cimic. clem.. *Colch.* coli. *Coloc..*
com. CON.. cot. croc. *Crot-t.* cycl. dream-p.
Dulc. euph. eupi. falco-pe. ferr. galeoc-c-h.
galla-q-r. gels. germ-met. gink-b. granit-m.
graph. grat. hell. *Helon. Hep.* hippoc-. hura
hydr. hyper. ind. indg. *Iod.* irid-met. kali-bi.
Kali-c. kali-i. kali-m. kali-p.. kali-sil. kola kreos.
lac-ac. *Lac-c.* lac-h. lach. *Lap-a.* laur. lavand-a.
led. lepi. lil-t. luna lyc. med. melal-alt. MERC..
Merc-d. merl. *Mez.* mim-p. mosch. murx. naja
nat-c. nat-m. nat-pyru. nit-ac. nux-m. nux-v.
ol-an. olnd. onos. orig. oxal-a. pall. pant-ac.
Ph-ac. Phel. Phos. Phyt. plat. plb. *Plb-i.* plut-n.
polyg-h. pot-e. prun. psor. puls. *Ran-s.* rheum_a.
rhod. *Rhus-t.* ruta. sabal sabin. sal-. sang. *Sec.*

sel. *Sep.* SIL.. spira. spong. stann. stram. stry.
Sulph. sumb. symph. syph. tab. tarent-c. thioc-
ac. thuj. tritic-vg.. tub. urol-h. vanil.. verat..
zinc. zinc-p.

425.   CHEST - PERSPIRATION - Mammae
arg-met. arn. bov. calc. fic-m. hep. kali-n. lyc.
plb. rhus-t. sel. sep.

426.   CHEST - PRICKLING - Mammae
arg-n. cimic.

427.   CHEST - PULSATION - Mammae
Bell.. borx. cench. *Phos..* symph..

428.   CHEST - RIVET or bullet; sensation of a -
Mammae; region of
lil-t.

429.   CHEST - RUBBING - Mammae
choc.

430.   CHEST - SEPARATED sensation - Mammae
separated from body
plut-n.

431.   CHEST - SMALL mammae
cham.. iod. lac-ac. lyc. nux-m.. onos. sabal
sulph.

432.   CHEST - SMALL mammae - one mamma is
smaller than the other
SABAL

433.   CHEST - SOFTNESS - Mammae; of
heroin. plut-n.

434.   CHEST - SWELLING - sensation of - Mammae
benz-ac. berb. calc-p. lach.

435.   CHEST - SWELLING - Mammae
aeth. all-s. anan. apis. arn.. ars-i. asaf. *Aster.*
aur-s. bamb-a.. *Bell..* bell-p. brom. *Bry..* bufo
Calc.. Carb-an. castm. *Cham... Clem.. Con... Crot-t.*

Cupr. cur. cycl. *Dig.* dream-p. *Dulc.* falco-pe.
ferr. graph. helo. *Helon. Hep.* heroin. hydrog.
irid-met. kali-c. kali-i. lac-ac. *Lac-c.* lac-h. *Lach.*
luna lyc. lyss. *Merc.* merc-c. *Merc-d.* merl. naja
nat-c. nat-m. oci. onos. oxal-a. pant-ac. *Phos.*
Phyt. pip-n. plb. psor. PULS. *Rhus-t.* ruta
sabad. sabin. sal-. samb. SIL. sol-a. sol-o.
spig. spong. *Sulph.* tarent. tritic-vg. tub. urt-
u. vip. *Zinc.*

436. **CHEST - TENSION - Mammae**
Bamb-a. Bry. cycl. kola puls. spong. tritic-vg.
vanil.

437. **CHEST - TICKLING in - Mammae**
sabin. sep.

438. **CHEST - TINGLING - Mammae in**
falco-pe. melal-alt. sabin. sal-.

439. **CHEST - TUMORS - Mammae**
aids. ars-br. ars-i. aster. *Bell.* berb-a. brom. bry.
calc. *Calc-f.* calc-i. calen. *Carb-an.* cham. chim.
clem. CON. *Cund.* ferr-i. gnaph. *Graph.* hecla
Hydr. Hyos. iod. kali-i. *Lach.* lap-a. lyc. merc.
merc-i-f. murx. nit-ac. osm. ph-ac. phel. *Phos.*
Phyt. plat. *Plb-i.* psor. *Puls.* sabin. sang. *Scir.*
Scroph-n. sec. *Sil.* skook. tep. thuj. thyr. tub.

440. **CHEST - TWITCHING - Mammae**
sulph.

441. **CHEST - ULCERS - Mammae**
alum. alum-sil. ars. ars-i. ars-s-f. aster. *Calc.*
calen. clem. *Hep.* hydr. kreos. *Merc.* paeon.
Phos. PHYT. SIL. sulph. thuj.

442. **CHEST - WARTS - Mammae; on**
castor-eq.

443. **BACK - PAIN - Dorsal region - Scapulae - left -**

extending to - Shoulder and mammae
grat.

444. BACK - PAIN - Dorsal region - Scapulae -
extending to - Mammae
grat.

445. DREAMS - CANCER - mammae
aster.

446. DREAMS - MAMMAE
Lac-e. lac-leo.

447. GENERALS - HISTORY; personal - cancer; of -
mammae; of
CON.

448. GENERALS - HISTORY; personal - mammae;
of recurrent inflammation of the
phyt.

- **Boger, C. M. – Synoptic Key**

449. MENSTRUATION - Concomitants before
menses - mammae
CALC. chin. CON. cycl. helo. kali-c. *Kreos.* lac-
c. merc. sang. spong.

450. MENSTRUATION - Concomitants during
menses - mammae
berb. *Bry.* CALC. *Carb-an.* CAUST. CHAM.
CON. *Dulc.* grat. HELO. IOD. LAC-C. *Merc.*
Murx. PHOS. PHYT. rhus-t. *Sang. Thuj.* vib.
zinc.

451. MENSTRUATION - Concomitants after
menses - mammae
Berb. cycl.

452. CHEST - Mammae - mammae
acon. alum. am-c. ambr. APIS ARN. ARS. *Asaf.*
bar-c. BELL. *Borx.* BRY. CALC. camph. CARB-

AN. carb-v. caust. CHAM. CLEM. cocc. *Coloc.* CON. croc. cupr. dig. *Dulc.* ferr. *Graph.* guaj. HEP. *Iod.* kali-c. *Kreos. Laur. Lyc.* mang. *Merc.* mez. nat-c. nat-m. *Nit-ac.* nux-m. nux-v. op. petr. ph-ac. PHOS. PHYT. *Plb.* PULS. ran-s. rheum *Rhus-t.* ruta *Sabin.* samb. *Sep.* SIL. SULPH. thuj. verat. zinc.

453. CHEST - Mammae - mammae - right
apis bell. borx. carb-an. con. murx. phel. sang.

454. CHEST - Mammae - mammae - left
calc. cist. fl-ac. lach. lil-t. sabad.

455. CHEST - Mammae - mammae - behind - right
am-m. lob.

456. CHEST - Mammae - mammae - behind - left
ant-t.

457. CHEST - Mammae - mammae - below
PHOS.

458. CHEST - Mammae - mammae - below - left
CIMIC. con. *Kali-c.* lach. mez. UST. visc.

459. CHILL - Partial chill - partial chill - on mammae
cimic. cocc. con. dig. guaj. nux-v. rhus-t.

460. CHILL - Partial coldness - coldness chilliness; sense of - partial - mammae
cimic.

- **Schroyens, Frederick - Synthesis 9.2.1b**
  461. MIASMS - cancerous miasm
acet-ac. acon. alum. alumn. *Ambr.* ANAC. anan. anil. *Ant-m.* anthraci. *Apis* apoc. arg-met. arg-n. ARS. ars-br. *Ars-i.* asaf. *Aster. Aur.* aur-ar. aur-i. *Aur-m.* aur-m-n. aur-s. *Bapt.* bar-c. bar-i. bell. bism. BROM. *Bry. Bufo* cadm-met. *Cadm-s. Calc.* calc-ar. *Calc-i.* calc-ox. *Calc-s.*

Calen. calth. *Carb-ac.* CARB-AN. *Carb-v. Carbn-s.* CARC. card-m. caust. chel. chin. chol. cholin. *Cic.* cinnm. *Cist. Cit-ac.* cit-l. clem. CON. conin. cory. crot-h. *Cund.* cupr. cupr-act. cur. dulc. echi. elaps eos. epiph. eucal. euph. euph-he. ferr-i. ferr-p. ferr-pic. form. form-ac. fuli. *Gali.* gent-l. ger. *Graph.* gua. *Ham.* hep. *Hippoz. Hydr.* hydrin-m. ign. *Iod.* iris *Kali-ar. Kali-bi.* kali-c. kali-chl. *Kali-cy. Kali-i. Kali-p. Kali-s. Kreos.* kres. *Lach. Lap-a.* lob-e. LYC. mag-m. maland. matth. med. *Merc. Merc-i-f.* methyl. *Mill. Morph.* mur-ac. murx. nat-c. nat-cac. nat-m. nectrin. NIT-AC. *Ol-an. Op.* orni. oxyg. ph-ac. PHOS. PHYT. pic-ac. plb-i. psor. rad-br. ran-b. rub-t. rumx-act. ruta *Sang.* sarcol-ac. *Scir.* scroph-n. sec. sed-r. *Semp.* sep. sieg. SIL. silphu. spong. squil. STAPH. stront-c. *Strych-g.* sul-ac. *Sulph.* symph. syph. tarax. tarent. tax. *Ter.* thap-g. *Thuj.* trif-p. viol-o. visc. *X-ray* zinc.

462. MIASMS - psoric miasm

abrot. acet-ac. acon. adlu. aesc. *Agar.* alco. aln. ALOE alum. alumn. am-c. am-m. ambr. amyg. anac. ang. anh. *Ant-c.* ant-t. apis aran. arg-met. arg-n. arn. ars. *Ars-i.* ars-s-f. asaf. asar. astra-e. aur. aur-m. bac. *Bar-c.* bell. benz-ac. berb. berb-a. beryl. bism. bor-ac. borx. bov. bry. bufo buni-o. CALC. calc-act. calc-f. *Calc-p.* calc-s. camph. cann-s. canth. caps. *Carb-an. Carb-v.* caust. cham. chel. chin. cic. cina cinnb. cist. clem. coc-c. coca cocc. coff. colch. coloc. con. cortiso. croc. crot-c. crot-h. *Cupr.* cycl. cyna. daph. des-ac. dig. dros. dulc. euph. euph-cy. euph-l. euphr. ferr. ferr-ar. ferr-ma. ferr-p. fl-

ac. flav. galph. graph. guaj. guat. halo. ham.
harp. hell. helon. *Hep.* hip-ac. hir. hist. hydr.
hydr-ac. hyos. hypoth. iber. ign. iod. ip. kali-
ar. kali-bi. *Kali-c.* kali-i. kali-n. kali-p. kali-s.
kreos. kres. lac-c. lac-d. lach. laur. led. levo. lil-
t. lob. LYC. m-arct. m-aust. *Mag-c. Mag-m.*
mag-s. mand. mang. *Merc.* merc-c. mez. mill.
mim-p. morph. mosch. mur-ac. murx. *Nat-c.*
Nat-m. nat-s. nicc. *Nit-ac.* nux-v. oci-sa. okou.
Ol-j. olnd. onop. op. orig. palo. par. paraph.
ped. perh. pers. *Petr.* ph-ac. phal. phenob.
phos. plat. plb. plb-act. pneu. podo. prot.
PSOR. puls. pyrog. ran-b. rauw. reser. rheum
rhod. rhus-t. rib-ac. rumx. ruta sabad. sabin.
samb. saroth. sarr. sars. sec. sel. seneg. sep. *Sil.*
spig. spong. squil. stann. staph. stram. stront-
c. sul-ac. SULPH. tarax. tarent. tell. teucr.
thala. ther. thiop. thuj. thyr. trif-p. trios. tub.
tub-r. ven-m. verat. visc. zinc.

463. MIASMS - sycotic miasm
adlu. aesc. *Agar.* agn. alum. alumin. alumn.
am-c. am-m. ambr. anac. *Anan.* ang. ant-c. ant-
t. *Anthraco. Apis* aran. ARG-MET. ARG-N.
arn. *Ars.* asaf. asar. asim. aspar. *Aster.* aur.
Aur-m. aur-m-n. *Bar-c. Benz-ac.* berb. berb-a.
borx. bov. bry. bufo calad. *Calc.* cann-i. cann-s.
canth. caps. carb-ac. carb-an. carb-v. carbn-s.
castm. caul. *Caust.* cedr. cham. chim. chin. cic.
cimic. cinnb. clem. cob-n. coc-c. coch. colch.
coloc. con. cop. croc. crot-h. crot-t. cub. cupr-
act. cycl. cyna. dig. dor. *Dulc.* epig. erech. erig.
ery-a. eup-pur. euph. euph-pi. euphr. fago.
Ferr. Fl-ac. flav. gamb. gels. gnaph. *Graph.* guaj.

guat. helon. hep. hydr. influ. *Iod.* kali-bi. kali-c. kali-i. kali-m. kali-n. KALI-S. kalm. kreos. kres. *Lac-c. Lach.* lil-t. lith-c. LYC. mag-c. *Mang. Med.* merc. *Merc-c.* merc-d. *Merc-sul. Mez.* mill. mosch. murx. nat-c. *Nat-m. Nat-p.* NAT-S. NIT-AC. nux-v. ol-j. orig-v. pall. pareir. penic. petr. petros. ph-ac. phos. *Phyt.* pic-ac. pip-n. plat. plb. pneu. prun. psor. puls. rat. rauw. rhus-t. sabad. SABIN. sacch-l. sanic. sarr. *Sars. Sec. Sel.* senec. seneg. SEP. *Sil.* spig. STAPH. still. stram. *Sulph.* tab. tell. ter. THUJ. thyr. uran-n. ven-m. vib. zing.

464. MIASMS - syphilitic miasm
aethi-a. aethi-m. agn. ail. allox. aln. am-c. anag. *Anan. Ang.* ant-c. *Ant-t. Apis* arg-cy. arg-i. arg-met. arg-n. arn. *Ars.* ARS-I. ars-met. *Ars-s-f. Asaf.* asar. *Asc-t.* astra-e. AUR. aur-ar. aur-br. aur-i. AUR-M. aur-m-k. AUR-M-N. aur-s. bad. bapt. bell. benz-ac. berb. berb-a. buni-o. cadm-met. calc-ar. *Calc-f. Calc-i. Calc-s.* calo. *Carb-an.* carb-v. carc. *Caust. Cean. Chim.* chinin-ar. chr-o. *Cinnb.* clem. cob-n. *Colch. Con.* convo-s. cop. cor-r. cory. crot-c. crot-h. cund. cupr. cupr-s. echi. ery-a. eryth. eucal. euph. ferr. ferr-i. *Fl-ac.* franc. *Graph.* gua. guaj. ham. hecla *Hep.* hip-ac. *Hippoz.* hir. hydr. hydrc. hypoth. iber. *Iod. Iris* jac-c. *Jac-g.* jatr-c. jug-r. *Kali-ar. Kali-bi.* kali-br. kali-c. *Kali-chl.* kali-f. KALI-I. *Kali-m.* KALI-S. *Kalm. Kreos. Lac-c.* lac-d. *Lach.* LAUR. *Led.* lith-c. *Lyc.* maland. med. MERC. merc-aur. MERC-C. merc-cy. *Merc-d.* MERC-I-F. MERC-I-R. *Mez.* mill. nat-s. nep. NIT-AC. nux-v. ol-sant. osm. penic.

perh. petr. petros. *Ph-ac. Phos.* PHYT. pilo. pitu. plat. plat-m. psor. reser. rhod. rhus-g. *Sabad. Sang. Sars.* sec. sel. *Sep.* SIL. spong. *Staph.* stict. STILL. strych-g. *Sul-i. Sulph.* SYPH. ter. thala. thiop. *Thuj.* thymol. *Thyr.* tub. ulm-c. vac. *Viol-t.* xan.

465. MIASMS - tubercular miasm
abr. acet-ac. AGAR. all-c. alum. alum-sil. alumn. ambr. ant-c. ant-i. ant-t. apis arg-n. ARS. *Ars-i.* ars-s-f. aur. *Aur-ar.* aur-fu. aur-i. aur-m. BAC. bapt. *Bar-c.* bar-m. bell. brom. bry. bufo CALC. calc-ar. calc-i. CALC-P. calc-s. calc-sil. calo. *Carb-ac.* carb-an. *Carb-v. Carbn-s.* carc. caust. cetr. cham. chin. chinin-ar. chr-o. cic. *Cist.* con. crot-t. cund. DROS. dulc. elaps euon. ferr-ar. ferr-i. ferr-p. ferr-pic. fl-ac. form. form-ac. gal-ac. graph. guaj. guar. guare. hep. hippoz. *Hydr. Hydrc.* iod. irid-met. kali-ar. *Kali-bi.* kali-c. *Kali-chl. Kali-i.* kali-m. kali-n. kali-p. kali-s. *Kreos.* lac-d. lach. lachn. laur. LYC. m-arct. med. merc. merc-i-r. myos-a. myric. nat-cac. nat-m. nat-s. nat-sel. *Nit-ac.* ol-j. ph-ac. phel. PHOS. *Phyt.* plb. polygn-vg. *Psor.* ran-b. rhus-t. sabin. sang. SANIC. scir. senec. seneg. sep. SIL. spong. stann. staph. sulph. syph. TARENT. ther. thiosin. *Thuj.* TUB. tub-a. tub-d. *Tub-k.* tub-m. tub-r. tub-sp. urea x-ray zinc.

Bibliography

1. Allen, H. C. - Keynotes and Characteristics with Comparisons of Some of The Leading Remedies
2. Allen, H. C. – Materia Medical of some important Nosodes
3. Allen, J. H., The Chronic Miasms, B. Jain Publishers (P.) Ltd., New
4. Banerjea, Subrata Kumar- Miasmatic Diagnosis, Revised Edition, 2003
5. Banerjee, D. D. (New Edition)- A Text Book of Homoeopathic Pharmacy- p. 47-50
6. Banerjee, S. K. - Miasmatic Diagnosis Practical Tips with Clinical Comparisons, B. Jain Publishers (P.) Ltd., New Delhi, Revised Edition 2003.
7. Benerjee, D. - The Glimpses of History of Medicine- p. 1, 4, 10-12, 14-15, 18, 21, 27, 33, 45, 49, 52
8. Bennet, Laurence - Clinical Pharmacology- p. 760, 769
9. Bennett, J. Claude, and Fred Plum, eds. Cecil Textbook of Medicine. Philadelphia: W. B. Saunders Co., 1996
10. Berkow, Robert, The Merck Manual of Medical Information, Merc & Co. In New York 1st Edition, 1999
11. Bernoville, Fortier - What We Must Not Do In Homoeopathy
12. Biller B. M. Hyperprolactinemia. Int. J. Fertil Womens Med. 1999; 44, 74- 77
13. Blackwood, A.– A manual of Materia Medica, Therapeutics and Pharmacology
14. Boericke, William - Pocket Manual of Homoeopathic Materia Medica & Repertory, B.

Jain Publishers (P.) Ltd., New Delhi, Reprint Edition 1999

15. Boerricke, Oscar - Repertory
16. Boger C. M., Boenninghaussen - Boger C. Boenninghaussen's Repertory
17. Boger, C. M. – A Synoptic Key of the Materia Medica
18. Borland, Douglas M. - Homoeopathy for Mother & Infant- p. 23, 25-26
19. Buckman M., Peake G. Untitled response to: Kemmann E. Incidence of galactorrhea [Letter]- JAMA 1976; 236:2747
20. Burnett, C. - The Change of Life in Women- p. 8, 15, 17, 34, 61-62, 66
21. Burt, W. H. – Physiological Materia Medica
22. Callen, Peter W., M. D. - Ultrasonography in Obstetrics and Gynecology
23. Chaddha, P. V. - Hand book of Experimental Physiology & Biochemistry
24. Chaterjee, Chandi Charan - Human Physiology, 11th Edition- p. 713, 716
25. Chaudhury, K. - Practice of Medicine- p. 38, 45, 49-51
26. Chauhan, Jahan Singh, Gynaecology, Cahukhamba Ayurvigyan Granthmala, Chaukhamba Surbharti Prakashan, Varanasi- Prasav Sambandhi Rog- p. 517
27. Choudhary, Harimohan - Indications of Miasm, B. Jain Publishers (P) Ltd., New Delhi, Reprint Edition 1994
28. Choudhury, N. M. - A Study on Materia Medica
29. Clarke, G. H., The ABC Manual of Materia Medica & Therapeutics

30. Clarke, J. H. - Clinical Repertory
31. Clarke, J. H. - Homoeopathy Explained, B. Jain Publishers (P.) Ltd. New Delhi, Reprint Edition 1995
32. Clarke, John Henry - A Dictionary of Practical Materia Medica (Vol. 1 to 3)- B. Jain Publishers (P.) Ltd., New Delhi, Reprint Edition 2000
33. Clarke, John Henry - Non Surgical Treatment of Diseases of the Glands & Bones with a Chapter on Scrofula
34. Clause, Stuart - The Genius Of Homoeopathy
35. Cowperthwaite, A. C. - A Textbook of Materia Medica & Therapeutics, B. Jain Publishers (P) Ltd., New
36. Cowperthwaite, A. C.- Text Book of Gynecology Delhi- p. 1, 394, 444, 469, 473, 484, 508, 595
37. Crooke, Stanley T., Archie W. Prestayko- Cancer and Chemotherapy Vol. I- p. 82
38. Crooke, Stanley T., Archie W. Prestayko- Cancer and Chemotherapy Vol. II- p. 105, 110, 115
39. Das, K. – Handbook of Surgery, 5th Edition- p. 151
40. Das, K.- Clinical Methods in surgery- p. 230
41. Davajan V., Kletzky O., March C. M., Roy S., Mishell D. R. The significance of galactorrhea in patients with normal menses, oligomenorrhea, and secondary amenorrhea. Am. J. Obstet. Gynecol. 1978; 130:894-904
42. Davidson's Principles and Practice of Medicine, Delhi, Reprint Edition, 1988- p. 424- 425, 427- 428
43. De Vries Herbert A. -Physiology of Exercise, 9th Edition- Chp. 9- p. 164
44. Dewey, W. A. - Essentials of Homoeopathic Therapeutics, B. Jain Publishers (P) Ltd., New

    Dr. Rajneesh Kumar Sharma

Delhi, Reprint Edition 1981
45. Diagnosis and Management of Galactorrhea -
August 1, 2004 - American physicians
46. Drug Today 2007
47. Dunn N. R., Freemantle S. N., Pearce G. L., Mann
R. D. Galactorrhoea with moclobemide [Letter].
Lancet 1998; 351:802
48. Edge D. S., Segatore M. Assessment and
management of galactorrhea. Nurse Pract.
1993;18:35-6, 38,43-4, passim.
49. Egberts A. C., Meyboom R. H., De Koning F. H.,
Bakker A., Leufkens H. G.- Non-puerperal
lactation associated with antidepressant drug use.
Br. J. Clin. Pharmacol. 1997 44:277- 281
50. Encyclopaedia Homeopathica, ver. 2.2.2 ,
2007/1/12- - Archibel, Belgium
51. European Journal of Classical Homoeopathy-Vol.
1- No. 1, Summer 1996, Ch.3, p. 3, Ch. 2, p. 325
52. Farrington, E. A. - Clinical Materia Medica
53. Farrington, E. A. - Comparative Materia Medica
54. Farrington, E. A. - Therapeutic Pointers
55. Faubion W. A., Nader S. Spinal cord surgery and
Galactorrhea: a case report. Am. J. Obstet. Gynecol.
1997; 177:465- 466
56. Fetrow C. W., Avila J. R. Professional's handbook
of complementary & alternative medicines.
Springhouse, Pa.: Springhouse, 1999:82- 83, 248-
249
57. Galactorrhea (Hyperprolactinemia). In
Professional Guide to Diseases. 5th ed.
Springhouse, P. A.: Springhouse Corporation, 1995
58. Galactorrhea- In Current Medical Diagnosis &
Treatment, 1998. 37th ed. Stamford: Appleton &

Lange, 1997
59. Galactorrhea- In The Merck Manual of Diagnosis and Therapy. 16th ed. Ed. Robert Berkow. Rahway, N. J.: Merck Research Laboratories, 1992
60. Ganong's Text Book of Physiology
61. Ghai, O. P. - Essential Pediatrics- 72, 338, 339, 342
62. Goodman & Gilman - The Pharmacological Basis of Therapeutics, Vol. I & II, 8th Edition.
63. Gray's anatomy
64. Gunavante, S. M. - The Genius of Homoeopahic Remedies
65. Gupta, A. C. - Organon of Medicine, At A Glance, Part I & II
66. Gupta, S. P., Dr. A. K. Gupta- Medical Emergencies In General Practice- p. 249
67. Guven K., Kelestimur F. Hyperprolactinemia and galactorrhea with standard-dose famotidine therapy [Letter]. Ann. Pharmacother 1995; 29:788
68. Guyton- Text Book Of Medical Physiology, 6th Edition- 702, 708, 916-929, 1001-1002, 1006-1015, 1035
69. Hahnemann, Samuel - Organon of Medicine, B. Jain Publishers (P) Ltd., New Delhi 6th Edition Reprint Edition 1996
70. Hahnemann, Samuel, The Chronic Diseases, Their Peculiar Nature & Their homoeopathic Cure, B. Jain Publishers (P) Ltd., New Delhi 5th Edition
71. Harrison' Principles of Internal Medicine, 11th Edition, Vol. I- p. 355, 401, 402, 430, 611, 871, 981
72. Harrison' Principles of Internal Medicine, 11th Edition, Vol. II- p. 1322, 1550, 1568-1567, 1569, 1589, 1649-1650, 1694- 1732, 1818-1819, 1837-1838, 1850

   Dr. Rajneesh Kumar Sharma

73. Haziq- p.135
74. Herbert A. Roberts- The Principles & Art of Cure by Homoeopathy
75. Hering, C., The Guiding Symptoms of our Materia Medica Vol. 1 to 10, Reprint Edition 1993
76. Homint R & D News Letter- 2/1999 p. 3
77. Homoeopathy in Thyroidism- The Similitude, vol. 1, No. 4, July 2000 - p. 17
78. Hoyne, T. S. - Clinical Therapeutics, B. Jain Publishers (P) Ltd., New Delhi, Vol. I & II, Reprint Edition 1993
79. http://www.aafp.org/afp/20010501/1763.html
80. http://www.healthline.com/galecontent/galactor rhea
81. http://www.merck.com/mmhe/sec13/ch162/ch1 62f.html
82. Hughes, R. and Dake J. P. - A Cyclopedia of Drug Pathogenesy
83. Jeby Haqeem, an Urdu Medical Book By Haqeem Mohammad Abdul Rehman, 28-04-1938 ed. – p.212
84. Julian, O. A. – Materia Medica of New Homoeopathic Remedies
85. Kanodia, K. D. - Danger Zones In Homoeopathy
86. Katsuren E., Ishikawa S., Honda K., Saito T. Galactorrhoea and amenorrhoea due to an intradural neurinoma originating from a thoracic intercostal nerve radicle. Clin. Endocrinol. [Oxf.] 1997; 46:631- 636
87. Katznelson L, Klibanski A. Hyperprolactinemia: physiology and clinical approach. In: Krisht A. F., Tindall G. T., eds
88. Kent, J. T. - Lectures on Materia Medica, B. Jain Publishers (P) Ltd., New Delhi

89.   Kent, J. T. - Repertory Of Homoeopathic Materia Medica

90.   Kent, J. T. - Repertory of the Homoeopathic Materia Medica, B. Jain Publishers (P) Ltd., New Delhi, Reprint Edition 2001

91.   Kent, James Tyler - Lectures on Homoeopathic Materia Medica

92.   Kleinberg D. L., Noel G. L., Frantz A. G. Galactorrhea: a study of 235 cases, including 48 with pituitary tumors. N. Eng. l. J . Med. 1977; 296: 589- 599

93.   Kruickshank, Robert - Handbook of Bacteriology, 10th Edition, 1960- p. 760- 761

94.   Kumar, Mittal- Basic Physics I & II

95.   Lee S. T. Hyperprolactinemia, galactorrhea, and atenolol [Letter]. Ann. Intern. Med. 1992; 116:522

96.   Lesser, O. – Text Book of Homoeopathic Materia Medica

97.   Lilienthal, S., - Homoeopathic Therapeutics

98.   Lippe, Adolph Von. – Key Notes and Redline Symptoms of the Materia Medica

99.   Lippe, Adolph Von. – Text Book of Materia Medica

100. Love and Baily – A Short Text Book of Practice of Surgery, 15th Edition- p. 269, 607- 635

101. Madlon-Kay D. J. 'Witch's milk.' Galactorrhea in the newborn. Am. J. Dis. Child 1986;140:252- 253

102. Magazine- S.K.H.M.C. Kanpur, 1972- 1973

103. Migael, A. Pagliarulo- Introduction to Physical Medicine- p. 233

104. Mohan, Harsh-Text Book of Pathology, Jaypee Bro. Medical Publishers (P) Ltd. 5th edition

105. Molitch M. E., Management of prolactinomas during pregnancy. J. Reprod. Med. 1999; 44:1121-

1126

106. Molitch M. E., Medical treatment of prolactinomas. Endocrinol. Metab. Clin. North Am. 1999; 28:143-169, vii.
107. Murphy, Robin - Lotus Materia Medica, B. Jain Publishers (P) Ltd., New Delhi, 2nd Revised Edition
108. Nash, E. B. - How to Take the Case & To Find the Similimum- p. 2- 14
109. Nash, E. B. - Leaders in Homoeopathic Therapeutics
110. Norman, L. Browse- An Introduction to the Symptoms and Signs of Surgical Diseases – p. 198, 199, 287- 308
111. P. V. S. N. Prasad - Homoeopathic Management of Surgical Cases - Souvenir State Homoeo Conference- 2000, Moradabad
112. Pandey, Gyanendra - Ashok Vaidya Visharad Guide- p. 295- 296
113. Park, E. & K. Park- Text Book of Preventive & Social Medicine
114. Parson's Diseases of Eyes, 12th Edition – p. 36, 52, 54, 55, 109, 114, 115, 248, 281, 310, 341, 296
115. Patel, R. P., Chronic Miasms in Homoeopathy & Their Cure
116. Phatak, S. R. - Concise Repertory
117. Phatak, S. R. – Materia Medica of Homoeopathic Medicines
118. Physicians' desk reference: companion guide. Montvale, N. J.: Medical Economics, 2000:1293, 1315, 1337
119. Pituitary disorders: comprehensive management. Baltimore: Lippincott Williams & Wilkins, 1999:189- 198

120. Pollock, Anshutz Edward - New Old & Forgotten Remedies, B. Jain Publishers (P) Ltd., New Delhi, Reprint Edition 1987

121. Purandare, N. - Menopause- Current Concepts – p. 39, 93

122. Purandare, N., Suvarna S. Khadilkar- Dysfunctional Uterine Bleeding- An Update- p. 1, 11, 17

123. Radar 9.2.1b and 10.0.017- Archibel, Belgium

124. Robbins & Cortan, Pathologic Basis of Disease, 7th Edition, p. 264- 265

125. Robert, Herbert A. - Sensations As If….

126. Romanes, G. J. - Manual of Practical Anatomy Vols. 1, 2 & 3- Vol. 2 p. 14, 15, 75, Vol.3 p. 54, 209, 210, 298, 299, 302, 311

127. Rothenberg R. E., La Raja R. D., Pryce E., Mueller S. C. Breast cancer and idiopathic galactorrhea. J. Med. Assoc. Ga. 1990; 79:363- 365

128. Sanfilippo J. S., Implications of not treating hyperprolactinemia, J. Reprod Med.- 1999; 449 (12 suppl.): 1111- 1115

129. Sankaran, P. - The Repetition of Doses

130. Schroyens, Frederick - Synthesis 9.2.1b

131. Schwabe, Willmar - Practical Homoeopathy in Every Day Medical Practice

132. Sharma, A. K. - Guide to Pathology- p. 179

133. Shaw's Text Book Of Gynecology- p. 690

134. Sircar, S. D. - Organon Expositor

135. Speight, Phyllis- A comparison of the Chronic Miasms B. Jain Publishers (P) Ltd., New Delhi, Reprint Edition - 1998

136. Sterility, Infertility, its investigations and Homoeopathic Treatment, R. R. Sharma- The Vital

Force, an Update- Souvenir, 1998, Lucknow
137. Stuart M., ed. The Encyclopedia of herbs and herbalism. New York: Grosset & Dunlap, 1979:176, 191, 239, 276- 277
138. Sukumaran, N. – Main Symptoms of Heart Problems
139. Taber's Cyclopedic Medical Dictionary
140. Taylor M. L. - Homoeopathy, Introductory Lectures
141. The Concise Oxford Dictionary
142. Tierney, Lawrence M., Stephen J. McPhee- Current Medical Diagnosis & Treatment- p. 728, 758- 760, 1051, 1054, 1059, 1072- 1074
143. Tolis G., Somma M., Van Campenhout J., Friesen H. Prolactin secretion in sixty-five patients with galactorrhea. Am. J. Obstet. Gynecol. 1974; 118: 91- 101
144. Tortora - Principles of Anatomy & Physiology
145. Turton D. B., Shakir K. M. Galactorrhea caused by esophagitis. Am. J. Obstet. Gynecol. 1995; 173: 1629- 1630
146. Verhelst J., Abs. R., Maiter D., Van den Bruel A., Vandeweghe M., Velkeniers B., et al. Cabergoline in the treatment of hyperprolactinemia: a study in 455 patients. J. Clin. Endocrinol. Metab. 1999; 84: 2518- 2522
147. Verma, P. N. - Materia Medica in Tabular Form
148. Vidyaratan- Handbook of Human Physiology- p. 246- 277
149. Virginia, A. LiVolsi, Maria J. Merino, John S. J. Brooks, Scott H. Saul, John E.- Pathology, 3rd Edition- p. 347, 349, 377, 378, 380, 391, 393, 398
150. Vithoulkas, G., - Materia Medica Viva

151. Vithoulkas, George - Science of Homoeopathy
152. Vodyazhina, I. - Text Book of Obstetrics- p. 26, 83, 175, 191, 194
153. Vol. I, II, III, IV, V, VI- Homoeopathic Pharmacopoeia of India
154. Vols. I, II & III- Synthetic Repertory
155. Voorthuisen, Van – A Text Book of Radio diagnosis- p. 158- 163
156. Vyas, Shiv Kumar - Ashok Ayurved Ratna Guide, 10th Edition- Vol. I p. 485, Vol. II p. 316
157. Weatherrall, Ledingham, Warrel, Oxford Textbook of Medicine, Oxford Medical Publications, 3rd edition
158. Windgassen K., Wesselmann U., Schulze Mönking H. Galactorrhea and hyperprolactinemia in schizophrenic patients on neuroleptics: frequency and etiology. Neuropsychobiology 1996- 33: 142- 146
159. World Homoeopathic Links, New Delhi, 2nd Edition, Reprint 1983
160. World Homoeopathic Links, New Delhi, 3rd Edition.
161. www.aafp.com
162. www.cancer.gov
163. www.cchindia.org
164. www.childbirthsolutions.com
165. www.daviddfriedman.com
166. www.emedicine.com
167. www.halta.org
168. www.healthonline.com
169. www.healthorg.com
170. www.hmc.org
171. www.homegci.net

 Dr. Rajneesh Kumar Sharma

172. www.hommiasm.com

173. www.homoeopathy.com

174. www.hpathy.com

175. www.library.med.utah.edu/kw/human_reprod/l ectures/clinical_genetics/index.html

176. www.medela.com

177. www.medsafe.govt.nz

178. www.pmjonline.com

179. www.qis.net

180. www.thenewmedicine.org

181. www.touregypt.net

182. www.whonamedit.com

183. Yarkony G. M., Novick. A. K., Roth. E. J., Kirschner K. L., Rayner S., Betts H. B. Galactorrhea: a complication of spinal cord injury. Arch. Phys. Med. Rehabil. 1992- 73: 878- 880

184. Yazigi R. A., Quintero C. H., Salameh W.A. Prolactin disorders. Fertil Steril 1997- 67: 215- 225

185. Yingling, W. A. – Accouncheurs Emergency Manual